What famous singers say about
Prima Donnas and Other Wild Beasts

Eileen Farrell—"It's delightfully entertaining and it shows how some of us have become victims of our own imagination. In reading it, I found myself laughing out loud."

Giorgio Tozzi—"A brilliant mosaic portrait of the opera star, skillfully wrought by one who loves not only the art in the artist but also the artist in the art."

Risë Stevens—"This book is highly amusing and most revelatory—and now I'm wondering to which category I belong—a Prima Donna or one of these beasts."

Eleanor Steber—"A charming and illuminating glimpse into the trials and tribulations of artistic greats. . . . I couldn't help but yearn for the days when a Prima Donna really was and not pretending to be. A primer for Prima Donnas—if they can get away with it."

ALAN WAGNER

PRIMA DONNAS AND OTHER WILD BEASTS

COLLIER BOOKS
NEW YORK, N.Y.

This Collier Books edition is published by arrangement with Argonaut Books, Inc.

Collier Books is a division of The Crowell-Collier Publishing Company

First Collier Books Edition 1963

Contents

Prima Donnas . . .

ONCE UPON a time, the great prima donna Emma Eames was singing the role of Elsa in Wagner's *Lohengrin*. In the second act, during the church scene, she got the notion that Katti Senger-Bettaque, who was playing Ortrud, was deliberately making a hash of accepted protocol by being out of her usual place in the wedding procession. So Eames hauled off and belted her in the chops.

When questioned about this public slapping, Senger-Bettaque remarked, "I did not resent it. I was really surprised and delighted to see *any* evidence of emotion in Madame Eames."

Score one for each side.

. . . and Other Wild Beasts

Prima Donnas and Other Wild Beasts

Chapter 1

Ars Gratia Artist, and Vice Versa

UNDER THE very best of circumstances, opera is a beautiful but irrational entertainment. It tends to resist the efforts of the statisticians and the rules-makers, thus maintaining its continuing vitality. Nowhere is the odd-ball nature of the art more apparent than in the antics of its favored few, the prima donnas. Which is fair enough, when you contemplate the fact that without them opera would be a faceless round of competence, unable to vie with the delights of the mass media.

Proponents of the "ensemble system," who usually tend to proliferate in companies that can't afford to pay prima donna fees, insist that the play's the thing, or should be, and that individual glamor must be subordinated to a sort of idealized anonymity. They translate "faceless" to read "selfless," and cloak the whole thing in a holier-than-thou rationale. What it all boils down to, of course, is a tranquil lake of mediocrity, undisturbed by storms or strange currents, but about as interesting as the Sargasso Sea.

Consider. Was it a new production of *Tristan und Isolde* at New York's Metropolitan Opera House in 1960 that drew capacity audiences and a front page review in *The New York Times,* or was it the local debut of a genuine star, Birgit Nilsson? Is it *ever* the production that is the cause of excite-

11

ment when the novelty wears off? Tebaldi or Callas are always news, no matter how shabby the sets around them, and it was true of Caruso and Tetrazzini and Melba and Patti and Grisi—back to the genesis of the art. You can often pick up decent tickets for a performance at any opera house, but try it when a star is announced, a real star.

Not only the production, but the very work itself is second in importance to the magnetism of the prima donna. Milan's famed La Scala opened its 1960–61 season with a deservedly obscure opera, Donizetti's *Poliuto*, which had been a more or less consistent failure at every one of its infrequent presentations including the first. Nevertheless, opening night seats were scalped at rates exorbitant even for Milan, international interest ran high, and the air in the theatre was charged with excitement. The cause was obviously not Donizetti's unattractive bomb, but the presence in the cast of Maria Callas. That by this time critics found her wide vibrato had become a full-fledged wobble and her top register a shrill shadow of itself was of no moment. What counted was that La Divina, a star if there ever was one, had made up her fight with La Scala's management and had returned To The Fold.

Callas, of course, is the mid-Twentieth-Century's front-page prima donna. Every epoch has one. When Rudolf Bing cancelled her Metropolitan Opera contract in 1959, it called for screaming headlines, not only in New York, and before and since she probably has gotten more newspaper column inches devoted to her than Adlai Stevenson and Elvis Presley combined. A tabloid serialized her mother's biography of her, gossip writers sniff at her trail when she boards Onassis' yacht, and whole cities hope breathlessly that she will either start or stop a feud with *their* opera company. Partisans for and against her art break out regularly into a rash of print, and wherever she and Management get together and she sings— there is honest theatrical excitement.

The virtues of Callas as an artist are wholly beside the point by now. She has metamorphosed from an Opera Singer into a Prima Donna; her presence on the scene injects continuing life into an endeavor that can all too easily get righteous and self-conscious.

What is true of La Divina is partly true of those few other genuine stars now in their prime: Renata Tebaldi, for example, whomps up a considerable stir whenever she sings and often when she doesn't. She and her contemporaries may not get the broad-based attention Callas attracts in non-operatic circles, but in the music world and its environs, among the aficionados and the plain garden-variety fans, a special kind of spotlight singles out the extraordinary from the usual, the star from the competent professional. The rewards of recognition are lavish and mutual.

It was ever thus. From Monteverdi to Montemezzi, the prima donna has generated unlikely enthusiasm. In 1884, the fabulous Adelina Patti was in San Francisco on tour with Colonel Mapleson's opera company. She had invariably sold out the house everywhere she had sung, but here she literally caused a riot. Or rather, a series of riots: from the moment she was announced, tickets were snatched up by speculators and were soon on sale throughout the city at prices ranging up to four hundred per cent of the face value. When these were gone, and only Mapleson's few remaining seats were left, sporadic mob scenes broke out at various advertised selling locations, places in line at the opera house were bought and sold like seats on the stock exchange, duels were threatened and perhaps even fought, and Mapleson himself was arrested for overcrowding the aisles at the theatre (a condition over which he had no control; the charge was settled by the magistrate in return for a season pass). The situation is perhaps most graphically described through contemporary eyes. Here is a part of the story as it appeared in the *San Francisco Morning Call* of March 15, 1884:

"To one who has stood on Mission Street, opposite the Grand Opera House yesterday afternoon and 'viewed the battle from afar' . . . it seemed that a large number of people had run completely mad over the desire to hear

Patti sing. Such an excited, turbulent, and, in fact, desperate crowd never massed in front of a theatre for the purpose of purchasing tickets . . . After the throng had melted away the approaches to the box-office looked as if they had been visited by a first-class Kansas cyclone in one of its worst moods. . . ."

And all for the sake of a pair of ducats to hear a soprano sing! Like most divas, Patti was perfectly well aware of the drawing power of her name, and would use all sorts of dodges to keep it that way. Among other things, she probably holds the all-time intercollegiate and AAU record for staging farewell performances, challenged only by Melba and Sarah Bernhardt. A statistics-minded reporter for the *Brooklyn Eagle* once figured that she had made her "last appearance" twenty-seven times; "positively last appearance" nine times; had "permanently retired from the stage" seven times; "retired to spend her days in her castle" three times; and, he concluded, was "now getting ready to take another hack at the public and retire again."

The point is, of course, that Patti is far from unique, whatever the extent of her legendary appeal. It is the star upon whom the public focuses—even *dotes*. Patti was neither the first nor the last, and if popular response is not always as rough-and-ready as in San Francisco's palmy days, it's nonetheless an awesome thing. As far back as 1757, over a century before Patti's prime, sophisticated Paris went wild over a young soprano who made her debut on September 15 of that year. She was the gifted Sophie Arnould, who later became as renowned for her wit as her voice, and mobs of Parisians, who supposedly should have known better, jammed her performances, thronged around the theatre, fought for seats. The contemporary observer Frèron said of the crowds: "I doubt if they would take such trouble to get into paradise." Those words could apply to a hundred cities, a hundred stars, many hundreds and thousands of audiences entranced by a similar spell, from that day to this.

"Prima donna." Literally "first lady," the phrase has by

accretion assumed a much wider implication. As a noun it has come to mean an opera singer of the female persuasion who transcends mere talent by the force of her personality, who has made of her idiosyncrasies a fine art, who generates a particular and immediately recognizable excitement whenever she appears. More and more in this country it has come to be applied even to baritones and tenors and basses, at least in an adjectival sense. Man or woman, the true opera star is the last of the Fabulous Beasts.

Giuseppe Verdi (or Gioacchino Rossini—the story has been ascribed to both, and it's apocryphal anyway) was once asked to list the three basic requisites of a great opera singer. He replied, "First, voice. Second, voice. Third, voice." Perhaps, but if the question read "star" instead of simply "singer," the Maestro—either Maestro—might have been forced to expand the answer. There *is* something else, something other than voice or musicianship or acting ability, some kind of chemistry that goes on when the audience knows it is face to face with a prima donna. Caruso, the most adored of tenors, possessed of a phenomenally beautiful voice, once tried an experiment to see how much of the adulation he was receiving was simple appreciation of artistry and how much was star-worship. Unannounced and unseen, he sang Beppe's serenade in Act II of Leoncavallo's *Pagliacci* as well as he knew how, without masking his own natural loveliness of tone. There was not a ripple of applause.

Of course, talent plays a key role in the creation of a star, especially talent with something of the spectacular about it. A good high E never hurt any career. Sometimes versatility helps, and sheer staying power (just recently Nell Rankin had six performances of three major roles plus rehearsals, in seven days, and in 1900 Ernestine Schumann-Heink sang three parts —Third Norn, Waltraute, and a Rhinemaiden—in one performance of *Götterdämmerung*). Nevertheless, the extra ingredient, lacking in the vast run of performers, is something extra-musical. It's been called temperament, and personality, and a couple of harsher things.

The chapters to come will of necessity confine themselves

to the telling of stories, stories revelatory of little more about the art of opera than the fact that it is practiced by some fairly unusual people, who face unusual problems and find unusual solutions. Opera is of course much more than that. For many it is even a central focus of life, and for many more it is the richest of all the arts. Among these the author numbers himself. Yet to smile at the foibles of a world is not to deny its worth. An opera-lover (and the word is singularly appropriate) is always perilously close to laughter as well as to tears; they both bespeak his deepest affection.

Chapter 2

So You Want to Be an Impresario

THE USUAL REACTION to the phenomenon of the prima donna ranges from fascinated interest to amused indulgence. There is one segment of society, however, that is so deeply affected by the whims and the talents of the stars that it hardly dares have any reaction at all: the segment occupied by the hard-pressed men who manage opera companies. Their destinies are inextricably bound up with the amount of money that comes in at the box-office window, and *that* figure, in turn, is wedded to the number, candle-power, and current well-being of the stars they can lure to their fold. Lure and keep happy, that is. The latter is practically a full time job, as witness the Metropolitan Opera executive who for years has called himself, unofficially, "Vice-President in Charge of Renata Tebaldi." Tebaldi, be it remembered, is not a particularly capricious diva, as divas go.

The necessity of keeping the box-office supplied with an influx of valid attractions is a real one; all talk about Art to the contrary notwithstanding, it has been and will always remain the key obligation of the opera manager. Nobody knew this better than the hard-headed genius of Sant'Agata, Giuseppe Verdi. When Giulio Gatti-Casazza was running the Teatro Communale of Ferrara, before his La Scala days, he presented Verdi's last opera *Falstaff*. After the opening he wired the old composer word of the opera's great success and added his own congratulations. Verdi telegraphed back: "Many thanks, but please inform me of receipts at the following performance."

In the pursuit of the star, impresarios have parted with vast sums of money and played all sorts of tricks. Often both have been needed. Legend has it that Oscar Hammerstein tried every gambit he could think of to get Nellie Melba to join his company, but the prima donna refused him regardless of the price. She was quite content in Paris, singing at the Opéra and carrying on a flirtation with the Pretender to the French Throne, Philippe d'Orleans. The wily showman would not give up, though. He insisted on seeing her once more at her suite at the Grand Hotel, offering her a fabulous fee if she would sign with him. Melba again declined. Hammerstein shrugged his shoulders, tossed a wad of thousand-franc notes into the air, and left. The money fluttered down all over the now laughing prima donna like so much confetti until the floor was strewn with what looked like a fortune. Dame Nellie signed up with Hammerstein the next day.

Opera singers have always had a healthy admiration for money, thrown into the air or however. The best of them earned fabulous fees and fought like cats to get them. What's more, once they had established a fee they protected it assiduously, serving as object lessons to our present-day stars.

One of the most adored prima donnas of the Nineteenth or any other Century was Adelina Patti, and during the greater part of her long career she was quite well aware of her worth. She figured it at approximately five thousand dollars a shot.

Five thousand dollars per performance may not seem astronomical in these days when a comedian can command five times that amount for a single television appearance, but it should be remembered, first, that Patti seldom sang before more than a couple of thousand customers, as opposed to the millions who watch any given TV program; second, the dollar went at least five times as far during her hey-day as it does now. For the period of Patti's ascendancy, five grand was a pretty monstrous salary, commanded by only the choicest few;

it would make almost any singer's mouth water even today.

Patti negotiated her huge fee with the impresario Colonel James H. Mapleson with an assist from a sister prima donna, Christine Nilsson, who later achieved an indelible immortality by singing Marguerite in the performance of Gounod's *Faust* that opened the Metropolitan Opera House. After a disastrous fire at Her Majesty's Theatre in 1868, Mapleson was rescued from the edge of bankruptcy by the appeal of Nilsson, his chief artist. While she was drawing the crowds to his company, Patti was the leading star and great attraction at the rival company at Covent Garden. Nilsson demanded, and got, whatever her rival got. Some years later, when Patti had become Mapleson's prima donna, Henry Abbey tried to entice her away to his opera group. In a counter-move Mapleson made overtures to his former star, Nilsson. The Swede, hearkening back to the days at Her Majesty's Theatre, insisted that she would sign for nothing less than whatever Patti's salary finally turned out to be. Mapleson, trapped, decided Adelina was the better drawing card of the two, bid her up to five thousand dollars a performance and thus away from Abbey, and for the moment Nilsson was left out in the cold.

That five thousand dollar figure remained an inviolable, almost sacrosanct, item with Patti. She would refuse to sing a note unless every penny of it was paid to her in advance. On one of the Mapleson tours of the United States, complete with gorgeously decorated private railroad cars for the star, she was scheduled to sing Violetta in *La Traviata* in Boston. Unfortunately, the impresario had run into a small streak of ill fortune and couldn't come up with her required fee before curtain time. The best he could do was four thousand. That was good, but not good enough, as the diva informed him. She would start dressing for the role but would leave off her shoes. Mapleson darted frantically away, returning a little while later with an additional eight hundred dollars in cash and a big smile. The smile faded as Patti condescended to put on one shoe only. Again he ran out. By now the audience had arrived and was beginning to get impatient. Finally, at the last minute, he breathlessly tore back into Patti's dressing room clutching the last two hundred dollars. The unperturbed diva calmly put on her other shoe, rewarded her manager with a queenly smile and swept on to the stage, where she gave a dazzling account of herself.

Sometimes the financial dealings between operatic artists and their employers (or prospective employers) can be pretty involved and complex, even a little weird. Francesco Tamagno, the trumpet-voiced tenor who created the title role in Verdi's *Otello*, was always in tremendous demand. He was appearing in Buenos Aires when Gatti-Casazza cabled an invitation for him to do *Otello* at La Scala during the 1898–99 season. Tamagno sent back a brusque demand for ten thousand lire per performance, with eight performances guaranteed and no quibbling allowed. The Scala board of directors was infuriated, as much by the tenor's curt attitude as by his unreasonable price. Arrigo Boïto, composer of *Mefistofele* and librettist for both *Otello* and *Falstaff*, was vice-president of the governing Council, and he was maddest of all. Not only was this an insult to the opera house and to himself, but to the great Verdi. He was certain that Tamagno's reply was the result of pique occasioned by the fact that Verdi had not interceded on his behalf with the French Government, which had been considering issuing a medal to the singer but had not yet done so. At any rate, Tamagno's name was dropped from further consideration, and the season's plans lined up without *Otello*.

Soon, however, La Scala found itself in unexpected difficulty. A projected new production of *Norma* that was to have been the focus of the season already underway had to be abandoned suddenly, and after the prescribed period of soul-searching it was again decided to approach Tamagno as a last resort. He was now back in Milan of his own accord, feeling a lot better about things in general because France had come through with the medal after all. He cheerfully offered to sing five performances of Rossini's *William Tell* for five thousand lire each. It wasn't the *Otello* that was hoped for, but Gatti concluded the deal with delight.

Rehearsals proceeded brilliantly. Tamagno was in his finest clarion form. All the greater was the shock, then, when on performance day the star's valet burst into Gatti-Casazza's office with the news that Tamagno had developed a bad cold. Gatti rushed to Tamagno's hotel, his season crashing in ruins before his eyes, to find that, sure enough, the tenor was miserably sick. His nose was so stuffed he was totally unable to sustain a tone (Tamagno, like many of the greatest tenors, produced his voice "into the mask"). Postponement was the only solution, one that Gatti reluctantly put into effect.

As soon as the postponement was announced rumors began flying around opera-happy Milan. Tamagno was old; he was tired. He was unable to sing the lyric *William Tell* because it was written for singers, not shouters. He had fought with Toscanini, the conductor. He had stage fright; he was terrified of losing his reputation at the hands of the critical Milanese. Tamagno, unaware of the comments his absence had spawned, remained in self-pitying and sniffy isolation until finally, on the third day, Gatti-Casazza could stand the delay no more. Judging his tenor correctly, the wily manager informed him that the people were saying that he was afraid, whereupon Tamagno exploded into a wild fury. His roars and shouts evidently cleared his nose and, after an experimental note or two, he haughtily informed all concerned that he would sing that very evening to teach these so-and-so Milanese a thing or two.

The word was spread. The thrown gauntlet, as much as the tenor's reputation and the mounting interest in the new production of *William Tell*, insured that La Scala was packed when the curtain went up that night. Tamagno's first entrance was greeted with a cold silence; nothing daunted, he proceeded to blast the audience with a fiery rendition of his opening aria "O Matilde, Io t'amo è vero." Excitement began stirring in the house. His second act allegro, "Al campo volo," was so enthusiastically applauded that it had to be repeated, and at the end of the act he was accorded an ovation which prompted him to wink at Gatti-Casazza and ask, "Eh? Isn't it true that the old man can still carry it off pretty well?"

Tamagno wasn't finished yet. In the last act he completely flabbergasted the now ecstatic crowd by lyrically singing the romanza "Oh muto asil del pianto" in a gorgeous *mezza voce*, following it before anybody could recover with a ringing and stentorian trumpeting of the succeeding cabaletta "Su corriamo." The demonstration afterwards, and again after the final curtain, was overwhelming. When the tumult finally died down and Tamagno was allowed to leave the stage, he turned, aglow with satisfaction, to the manager and said, "I do hope these big asses will be ashamed to have thought that I was frightened. And now, Gatti, I promise you that next season, if you wish, I shall sing *Otello*."

In case you'd forgotten, that was precisely what Gatti-Casazza had wanted all along.

Fiscal maneuverings are bad enough when everybody understands what everybody else is talking about. They can get downright dangerous when an element of uncertainty is added to the proceedings. From 1911 to 1919 the management of London's Covent Garden opera was in the dynamic if cantankerous care of Sir Thomas Beecham, the brilliant conductor and musical gadfly who died early in 1961. His regime, while it saw a number of notable "firsts," was not distinguished by any remarkable equanimity or self-restraint. Things kept happening to Sir Thomas, or vice-versa, to the extent that his total expenditures for opera were once estimated at over one million pounds sterling. He himself would never confirm the figure except to say, "When I heard it I fainted and had to be revived with brandy." It was early in his career as an impresario that Beecham found himself in the middle of a monetary squabble with the memorable Russian basso, Fyodor Chaliapin, whom he had brought to London. Surprisingly enough, his role was almost that of an innocent bystander, an unusual posture for Sir Thomas.

It was 1912. Beecham was presenting Chaliapin in a special performance of Mussorgsky's *Boris Godunov* for the Royal family, and apparently the basso had promised to divide his salary for the night among the Russian members of the troupe. True or not, a squabble arose within the Slavic contingent, and when Beecham arrived at the opera house during the supposedly spectacular Coronation Scene he found the stage absolutely empty except for Chaliapin and a couple of frightened-looking English choristers he had hired to help fill up the stage picture. There wasn't a Russian to be seen except for the Czar. As soon as the scene ended Beecham hurried backstage, where a monumental argument was in progress. The chorus, ballet, and principals were all gesticulating wildly and shouting at each other in Russian. Beecham finally managed to disentangle a few disputants who, via elaborate interpretation, conveyed that the fight was between Chaliapin and the chorus. The only man who might have been able to solve the argument, the Russian manager of the troupe, had fled the scene.

With considerable expenditure of energy Sir Thomas managed to herd the Russians back onto the stage, enabling the performance to continue, but it was a temporary victory. They were soon back at it again. This time Chaliapin himself and the leader of the chorus had a few words, ending in the basso knocking his opponent to the floor, whereupon he was surrounded by the whole infuriated chorus brandishing the staves they were to carry in the next scene. The noise rose to bedlam levels, and Beecham did what any sensible man would do under conditions of incipient riot: he laid low until the cops arrived. And arrive they did, a whole troop of bobbies, waving their sticks and blowing whistles. Chaliapin retired to his dressing room in somewhat tattered but still regal splendor behind a cordon of policemen while the harried Beecham persuaded the chorus to finish the opera by promising mediation.

Although ruffled, the choristers acquitted themselves nobly up to the final curtain, but then they absolutely refused to leave the stage until they had it out with Chaliapin. He finally emerged from his imperial dressing room, still surrounded by cops, carrying a loaded pistol in each pocket of his royal costume. By now the crowd, under Beecham's mollifying influence, was somewhat calmer, and the discussion proceeded in a comparatively orderly fashion. Beecham, his staff and the police could of course understand nothing that was said, but they were all enthralled by the sight of the star in his

Czar's robes and the chorus in their peasant costumes holding parley. First the leader of the chorus made a long sad speech, which was answered by a longer one from Chaliapin; a female chorister was next, followed again by a rebuttal from the basso. His last speech was capped by a huge joyous yell from the assembled Slavs, he was hugged and kissed by the entire chorus and all the principals, male and female, and a frenzied celebration of whatever it was that had just happened began. Chaliapin, signaling for silence, started a speech that was obviously in praise of Beecham, who began inching towards the door, as he had no great desire to be kissed by a horde of bearded Russian singers. Before the grinning crowd could descend upon him he slipped out the stage door with the cops right behind him, but the Russians stayed at the theatre partying until 5 A.M., breaking into the refreshment booths and brewing tea and coffee. They all showed up for rehearsal the next morning promptly, unconcerned, for all the world as if nothing whatever had happened the night before.

Chaliapin's difficulty with his colleagues, though not usual, is not unique. When Luisa Tetrazzini was in Uruguay, the orchestra refused to play unless she doubled their salary out of her own pocket. Never one to be bullied, the coloratura waited until curtain time, then appeared before the audience and announced that the scheduled opera could not be given because of the orchestra's demands. The disappointed spectators urged, as she knew very well they would, that she sing *without* the orchestra, and after a becoming show of reluctance she agreed. The performance, accompanied by a piano and solo violin, was a spectacular success.

Normally, however, the antagonists in any financial skulduggery are the singer on one hand and the manager on the other. It has always been thus. When it comes to money the two parties seem to be natural enemies, like the mongoose and the snake; which one is which depends on your primary allegiance. Prima donnas have been using all their wiles to get their fees raised, and sometimes just to get their fees, since opera's earliest days. In 1705, the English soprano Mrs. Tofts refused categorically to sing for impresario Rich because he withheld her salary when she cancelled because of a loss of voice due, she claimed, to Rich forcing her to sing three times a week in hot weather. Mrs. Tofts' unwillingness was genteel: often the refusal to sing comes at the damnedest places.

In the 1880's a troupe calling itself The Milan Grand Italian Opera Company was appearing in Chicago. The star of the company was Eva Cummings, whose best role was the lead in *Lucia di Lammermoor*. On one particular evening things progressed in an orderly fashion until the orchestra played the cue for the heroine's big Third Act entrance. Cummings didn't appear. The chorus milled about on the stage in a nonplussed sort of way as the orchestra suppressed a wave of chortles and the audience grew restless. Still no Cummings, until finally the curtain was lowered. Signor Alberto Sarata, the manager of the company, came forward to announce that the soprano had suddenly become quite ill, too ill to continue, but that the opera would proceed without her. At precisely this moment the absent Miss Cummings suddenly appeared at the embarrassed impresario's side and announced that she was in positively radiant health. All she wanted, she insisted, was her salary. The audience was divided, half cheering her and half hissing. Cummings bowed solemnly to one side of the house, then to the other, and was about to follow her departed manager off the stage when she discovered that the curtains were being held tightly shut from behind. Flashing a smile at the audience, she walked with dignity to one of the wings, only to discover that the curtain was tightly shut there, too. She darted to the opposite wing. That also was held fast. By now her smile had turned to panic as she skipped from exit to exit in solitary splendor. To the intense amusement of the hysterical spectators she found them all shut tight. "I will get off this time anyhow!" she cried, and charged at the center opening in the curtain like a young bull. The draperies resisted for a moment, then gave way, sending the prima donna sprawling backstage. When the hilarity had subsided, the curtain rose on the final scene of the work, with Edgar of Ravenswood mourning the death of a Lucy who, this evening, had not exactly died, much as she might have liked to.

Cummings' Last Stand, and its many sister demonstrations, have had their effect on the habits of even the greatest of the great. Lilli Lehmann was singing in London in Wagner's *Tristan und Isolde* in 1885 with Gudehus as her tenor. During the love duet in Act II he whispered to her that he would not continue with the performance until he got paid. She whispered back that for the sake of Art, Wagner, and Lehmann's formidable wrath he'd damned well better continue, at least until the end of the act. He did, but the intermission seemed interminable as Gudehus waited out his paycheck. It finally arrived, all right, and the show went on. Madame Lehmann wisely insisted upon payment in advance, in cash, for the rest of the engagement and almost always throughout her career.

Money as much as pique was responsible for the spectacular walkout from the Met staged by another great Wagnerian, the American Lillian Nordica. The season of 1897 had failed, under Abbey and Grau's joint management, despite such stars as Nordica, Emma Eames, Melba, Calvé, Scalchi, both de Reszkes, and Plançon, with Nordica winding up a creditor to the tune of about five thousand dollars. Under the reorganization that followed she forgave all and cheerfully accepted a fee of eleven hundred dollars as her part in keeping the company going. She was shocked, however, when she shortly discovered that Melba got twelve hundred, Calvé fourteen hundred, and Jean de Reszke twelve hundred plus a percentage of the receipts. The last straw was added when it was announced that Melba was going to sing Brünnhilde in *Siegfried*, a role Nordica considered personal property. Utilizing the ultimate weapon of the prima donna, she stalked out of the Met.

Amidst the monetary haggling that is usually characteristic of singer-manager relationships, the fact that Caruso, one of the most fabulous box-office attractions of all time, refused to accept *more* than twenty-five hundred dollars for any of his Metropolitan appearances is cause for wonder, and perhaps gives a clue to part of his greatness. He was offered more, even by the Met, but consistently stayed at his customary fee. One story has it that the tenor was offered a contract with the space for the amount of payment left blank; along with it came assurances that the Board would go as high as four thousand. Caruso said that no singer was worth such a figure. "If I ask for one cent more than twenty-five hundred dollars the public, one way or another, will find out and want from me that one cent more of singing which I have not got." His fee was established at the level he desired.

It is further said that prior to one season Caruso informed Gatti-Casazza, then managing the Metropolitan, that Hammerstein had offered him five thousand dollars per appearance. Gatti said that he would meet Hammerstein's figure rather than let Caruso go, but that he'd have to economize elsewhere by hiring second-rate conductors and colleagues. Caruso said, "I *insist* that you pay me only twenty-five hundred dollars."

It was not that the golden-voiced tenor was unaware of either his talents or the value of money. Call it responsibility, if you will. Certainly early in his career he had many brushes with hunger, enough to teach him the hard lessons that most stars never forget. As a matter of fact, he was almost lost to the Metropolitan completely because of pressing need. Maurice Grau had gotten the young Neapolitan to agree to sing in New York in the 1899–1900 season for two hundred dollars a week over a twenty week period but the impresario vanished from the area before anything was signed, and Caruso finally decided to go to St. Petersburg, the old Russian capital, instead. "I've waited long enough. I must have a new overcoat for the winter and some coal for my fireplace."

It was during that same year, 1899, that Caruso sang at Genoa with the superb baritone Giuseppe de Luca. They were both acutely poor, but would nevertheless eat out whenever they could scrape together the funds. One evening at the Righi Ristorante they were recognized by the proprietor, who made a big fuss over them and, inevitably, asked them to sing. Being young and full of good spirits, good food, and good voice, they obliged. Caruso started with the Flower Song from *Carmen* and then, sticking to Bizet, they did the big duet from *The Pearl Fishers*. The customers loved it. The artists were showered with applause, toasts were proposed by the beaming host: everything seemed to be on a beautifully friendly basis, until suddenly Caruso and De Luca were presented with a bill for 180 lire. The singers were shocked. Hadn't they just provided a marvelous show for the cafe's clientele? After talking it over, they informed the owner that their usual fee for a concert like the one they just gave was 300 lire. However, as they had consumed 180 lire worth of food and wine, they would be glad to settle matters if they were paid 60 lire apiece. There is no record of the outcome.

Later in his career, as his value to operatic entrepreneurs soared, Caruso was quick to take advantage of it. With the exception of the Metropolitan, his artistic home, he made few concessions, except to please a friend. Such a friend was baritone Antonio Scotti, perhaps the tenor's dearest companion and a first-rate artist in his own right. Scotti had gone from his initial success at La Scala (where he debuted as Hans Sachs in Wagner's *Die Meistersinger*, transalpinized as "Maestri Cantori") to Covent Garden in London, where he enjoyed similar triumphs. Higgins, the director of Covent Garden, deputized Scotti to try to hire his friend Caruso for a few appearances at eighty pounds apiece. Eighty pounds was then worth about two thousand lire, and when Scotti finally got up enough nerve to broach the matter, the tenor became furious at being offered a fee so far below his norm. It took some doing, but the baritone did talk him into coming to London, mostly by relying on the tried-and-true old formula, "If you haven't sung at Covent Garden you are not yet a star." Although he fulfilled that initial contract, Caruso did it with rather ill grace. It all culminated one afternoon when he collared his home-town colleague and roared, "You low Neapolitan! You have dragged me here at the salary of a baritone!"

If you think prima donna interest in salary is strictly from pre-AGMA days, there are dozens of stories to the contrary. One of the most recent concerns Birgit Nilsson. She was having a piano rehearsal of *Tristan und Isolde* in Vienna under the direction of Herbert von Karajan, the conductor and Artistic Director of the Vienna State Opera whose influence is so great he has been referred to as "Herr General Music-Director of Europe." Midway through, a string of her pearls broke and Karajan, helping to retrieve them, asked if they were "stage jewelry, or are they real pearls bought from your phenomenal Scala fees?"

Nilsson replied, "Oh no, these are cheap and very ordinary pearls bought from your Vienna fees."

The troubles that beset impresarios are not always fiscal. Far from it. Because so much of their success depends on the continued happiness of a clatch of pretty willful individuals they often must combine the qualities of a career diplomat, a nursery school teacher, and Billy Rose, and leaven it all with the patience of Job. No matter how well they plan, things all too often "gang agley." Colonel Mapleson, one of the most successful and most put-upon managers of all time, tried to leave as few things to chance as possible. Sometimes his foresight worked, as when he hired twenty-five "hoary-handed" boatmen to applaud at Christine Nilsson's London debut (in *La Traviata*), paying them one shilling apiece for every time they clapped loud enough to get the curtain raised for another bow after Act I. Sometimes, though, nothing worked.

There was the bitter occasion, for example, when he went all out to arrange a big welcome for Adelina Patti's 1883 arrival in New York. It was going to be one of the most spectacular greetings the harbor had ever seen, including a fleet of sixteen tugboats, a whole herd of military bands, a twenty-one-gun salute, and a special cantata to be sung in her honor. All the details were seen to, everything was ready, nothing was left to chance. The only thing was, nobody remembered to watch for Patti's ship. It slipped majestically past the pre-arranged signal point completely unobserved. The prima donna landed and instead of the anticipated furor there wasn't a soul there to meet her. She stood forlornly next to her baggage for a while until by sheer chance a friend of hers happened to drive by, picked her up and deposited her unceremoniously at her hotel in a plain utilitarian four-wheeler. Patti later claimed to the mortified Mapleson that she was just as glad, but the impresario was out the price of sixteen tugs, some military bands, a brace of cannons and a useless cantata.

One of the more hazardous tasks facing the managers of large opera companies is the yearly necessity of setting up the repertoire and assigning the leading roles. It's a lead-pipe cinch that very few of his stars will be pleased with the way he works things out. They all want the broadcast perform- ance, or the first performance (which the critics attend), or the new production. They love one role, hate another, must sing Wagner, cannot bear to sing Wagner. They must sing in February, but cannot in March. . . . The ramifications are endless, and the net result is that the impresario winds up being a heel to everybody, the one part he himself wants most to avoid. It's somewhat easier in this jet age, especially as opera singers are more accustomed to the necessities of inter- national schedule-building than they once were, but when Giulio Gatti-Casazza first arrived at the Metropolitan the dangerous custom existed of planning each week's repertory and casts on the previous Monday. More often than not singers would come barging into his office to see what he was doing and to voice their own demands. On one memorable occasion he had to do the best he could with *three* prima donnas hovering over his shoulder, one with her secretary, one with her mother, and the third with her husband. All six would shriek at him, clutch at the paper, pound the desk in fury. It was probably during those early painful days that Gatti decided he had enough trouble being yelled at in Italian, so why bother learning to speak English? One lan- guage was sufficient unto the day.

It was during these times as well that Gatti became sick of the constant pressure exerted on him by the singing teachers of various artists, all with a stake in their protégés' success. When somebody later asked him who was a good voice teacher, he replied, "That is an easy question. It is that teacher who is lucky enough to have an exceptional pupil."

Gatti-Casazza, of course, weathered the storms of his career better than most. He was a very resourceful gentleman. He was even said, by Geraldine Farrar, to keep two complete sets of books. One he showed to singers who requested raises. The other was shown only to members of the Board of Directors who wanted reassurances of solvency.

If casting in the aggregate is a problem, it's not as painful as the constant necessity of facing individual difficulties. In 1911, Sir Thomas Beecham presented a Mozart season at His Majesty's Theatre which he was quite anxious to cast as strongly as possible. Then as always the iconoclast, he went outside opera to sign someone for a lead, a favorite part, in one of the works. This young lady was quite well-known for her work on the musical comedy stage, where Sir Thomas had seen and admired her, but this was her first brush with the Finer Things. After a few pleasant and useful rehearsals, Beecham was visited by a male relative of his discovery, who announced that the soprano wanted to be relieved of her assignment. The astonished conductor asked, "Doesn't she like it?"

"Oh, she likes it well enough, but we both feel you have not been quite frank with us about it."

Sir Thomas was flabbergasted. "What do you mean?"

"Well, you told us that it was the principal role in the opera."

"Isn't it?"

"How can it be when it is written only on the second line?"

As calmly as he could under the circumstances Beecham pointed out such great parts as Carmen, where the music is on the third line, but to little effect. "That's all very well for people who understand these things," his visitor told him, "but you see Miss X has had a distinguished career in her own way and it might do her no end of harm in that world if it ever became known that she had ever sung anything else but the top line."

Beecham had no choice but to release her.

More usual, of course, is the prima donna who wants to sing a role that she is being denied or to branch off into new vocal territory. Olive Fremstad was for years the mainstay of the Metropolitan's Wagnerian wing, but she kept complaining to Gatti-Casazza that all these Kundrys and Brünnhildes and Isoldes and Venuses were too heavy and demanding. The General Manager assigned her Tosca, but the complaints continued until finally he offered her Giulietta in Offenbach's *The Tales of Hoffmann* which was going to be given for the first time at the Met during the 1911–12 season. She asked for a copy of the score, examined it carefully and then said, "Giulietta is a courtesan. I can take the roles of courtesans written in the heroic vein, but this Giulietta is too modern for me."

"Look here, Madame Fremstad," said Gatti, "now that I have found the part for you, something you have been asking for, you create difficulties."

The prima donna bristled. "Very well," she said coldly, "if you wish, I will sing it."

She did, too, and for the first time in her career she got bad reviews in the press. After two performances she approached Gatti-Casazza again and told him, "It's true that I am earning my pay in something that is not exhausting, but I do not like the idea of being roasted every time. Let me sing in something else."

"If I make the change, will you stop complaining?"

"Yes, yes, I promise I will never complain again even if roles are heavy."

The cast was duly changed, and the truce between the manager and the star remained in force. One night, some time later, Gatti arrived at the opera house to find the entire place in an uproar. It seemed that Maria Duchène, who was to sing Giulietta that night, had gotten stuck in an elevator that would go neither up nor down, and there was no replacement anywhere around. Desperate situations call for desperate measures, and the manager, gritting his teeth, phoned Fremstad at her home:

"I'm almost afraid to ask, because, though you are a fine woman, you are difficult . . . ," he began.

"Who says so?" she interrupted. "What makes you think so? Tell me what you want!"

Gatti told her the story of Duchène's inextricability.

"Very well, to show you I'm not difficult, I'm coming immediately to the Metropolitan!"

It was a wild dash, but she made it to the theatre in time to sing.

Two days later Fremstad was handed a check to cover her fee for the extra performance. She stormed into Gatti's office, flinging the check dramatically onto his desk. "No check!" she cried; "*that* to teach a lesson to the director who thinks I am a difficult woman. I will not take a cent!"

The whole affair was one that Gatti loved to recall in his later years. It marked one of the few complete tactical triumphs in his genial war with prima donnas.

Incidentally, it should be noted that during the following season the role of Giulietta was taken by the soprano Frances Alda, who was then Madame Gatti-Casazza. Alda was not exactly subtle about her desire to sing the part: at one rehearsal of *The Tales of Hoffmann,* during Act II, Fremstad as the courtesan was reclining on a couch on stage while her secretary was standing in the wings holding her dog Mimi. Alda wandered over and asked to pet the animal, but released it instead. The pooch dashed to Fremstad's couch, breaking up the rehearsal completely, while Alda strolled amiably away.

Fremstad was another pay-as-you-go prima donna: under normal circumstances, her check had to be handed to her before she'd go on stage, although the treasurer, perhaps with memories of Patti, would never give it to her until she was fully costumed and ready to appear. And her secretary, far from being able to carry dogs during performances, used to stagger around the wings burdened down by glasses of water, handkerchiefs, tins of jujubes, a hand mirror, complexion brush, throat spray and cashmere shawl, all of which Madame Fremstad might demand at her next exit.

Firing personnel is never a pleasant task, but never more painful than when the artistic temperament is involved. Early in the career of Giulio Gatti-Casazza he was the General Manager of the opera house in Ferrara, Italy, a tenure that led directly to his engagement at La Scala. One of his new productions there was Wagner's *Lohengrin,* dear to Gatti's heart, but the early rehearsals were dreadful, and they got steadily worse. Finally he could stand no more and made a clean sweep: Elsa, Lohengrin, Telramund, and the Herald all got the axe, which left him with Ortrud, King Henry, and a swan. The energetic young Gatti went out and rounded up a new cast, whipping them into reasonable shape in time for the first performance, but his trouble was not confined to the stage alone. The mother of the dethroned Elsa collared him in the lobby of the theatre, and cried, "You, Signor Gatti-Casazza, you have turned my hair gray. You see, don't you, I have had to have my hair dyed blonde. This cost me a large sum of money. If you were a gentleman and an honest man, you'd at least pay my expenses."

Even this appeal to his better instincts wasn't quite as harrowing as his encounter with the disenfranchised Herald, a huge, black-bearded baritone. "Don't you know that I have lost my parents?" he demanded of the cornered Gatti. "You are therefore responsible for having ruined the career of a poor little orphan!"

All in all, Regina Pinkert was acting in an old tradition when Oscar Hammerstein fired her after his first season. She screamed, ran around the room, fainted, got hysterical in a wide variety of ways, and in general made a rather memorable event out of her leaving, if not her stay.

Once in a while an impresario has the reverse problem, trying to convince a recalcitrant artist to sing. Often prima donnas are extremely opinionated about the roles they feel are right or wrong for them, resisting fiercely and heroically any attempts to convince them otherwise. Marianne Brandt, while at the Berlin Opera, was offered the opportunity to create the role of Leah in Anton Rubinstein's *Maccabaer,* an opportunity she vehemently rejected. Pressure was brought to bear from a number of quarters until she consented at least to learn the part, but matters got even more miserable during rehearsals. Brandt would cry and scream that "this role is a nail in my coffin." It took the combined efforts of most of the Opera staff and Rubinstein himself to get her on stage for the premiere, from which time on Brandt managed to sing the role with great success over fifty times, suffering no apparent damage to the voice. Leah was the making of her career in Berlin.

Opera is ideally a blend of music and theatre. Its theorists from Gluck to Wagner to, say, Joseph Kerman, have all been concerned with opera as drama, and it's probably true that more attention is paid to acting and the stage picture now than formerly. Prima donnas, though, have historically had a majestic disregard for such picayune details, with only a handful of today's luminaries being exceptions to the general rule. Integrated productions are occasionally achieved at the big cosmopolitan houses, but only at the expense of much whip-cracking and cajoling of the stars involved. For a recent and much-praised revival at the Metropolitan the leading lady hardly appeared at a single rehearsal, her understudy filling in for her right through dress rehearsal, whereupon she triumphantly resumed her role in time for the opening. Nonetheless, as bad as it can still sometimes be, it's nothing like the good old days.

Adelina Patti not only would never show up for rehearsals, but had her right to be so absent guaranteed her in her contracts. There were times during her historic touring days with Mapleson's company that she would not even have met her fellow-artists before performance time. At one *Il Trovatore*, for instance, the baritone asked for the honor of an introduction to Patti while singing in the first act trio. The tenor that evening, a polite and resourceful performer, managed to sing the formal introductions as part of his role.

Obviously, Patti didn't concern herself much with acting, any more than did the vast majority of her contemporaries. The description that has come down to us of her final moment in *Aida* tells the whole story. This is the marvelous scene in which Verdi's heroine, the Egyptian slave-girl Aida, hides in a dungeon in which her lover, Radames, is to be buried alive, so that they may at least die together. It's a poignant and touching finale to a stirring work, but not the way Patti played it. Just before the closing duet, "O terra addio" ("Farewell, O Earth"), she would punch up a pre-arranged sofa-cushion into a comfortable puff, kick her slim high-heeled Paris shoes around until she got her long train adjusted properly, settle slowly down onto her cushion with the aid of her tenor, get into a good relaxing position, and, more or less, die.

Even those stars with reputations for acting skill often cared a great deal less about the performance as a whole than about their own central place in the scheme of things. Fyodor Chaliapin was notoriously late for rehearsals, and not particularly cooperative when he did arrive. He cannot be said to have been overly popular with his lesser colleagues. Typical perhaps was his tardy entrance into a Met rehearsal, muttering to himself. Then, perhaps noticing the air of disapproval hovering around him, he said aloud in French, a language understood by everybody present, "Do you call this a temple of music? This is a stable, not a temple!"

Headstrong singers can be such a trial during rehearsal periods that it sometimes seems the lesser of two evils to accept gracefully the Patti concept of preparation-in-absentia. Albert Niemann, the great Wagnerian tenor, was scheduled to create the title role in Wagner's *Rienzi, the Last of the Tribunes* for the Royal Opera of Hanover during the 1860's. Rienzi's first entrance was supposed to be on horseback, and despite impassioned pleas Niemann insisted that the only horse he would deign to ride was a pure white charger that King Ernst of Hanover himself liked to ride daily through the streets of the city. The horse was almost as well known to the Hanoverians as King Ernst himself, but Niemann halted all preparations by insisting, "Either I ride the King's horse, or I do not ride at all."

This last alternative was not wholly unattractive to the hard-pressed manager. Nevertheless, he passed on Niemann's demand to King Ernst. Luckily, His Majesty was both easygoing and musical (he was the patron of the remarkable violinist Joachim) and readily agreed that the tenor could use the horse at the performance. Niemann, however, wasn't through yet. He said that if he was going to ride this animal on stage, an animal with which he was totally unfamiliar, he would have to rehearse with it. Not on stage, mind you: he'd have to be able to ride him around town for a few hours a day on each of the four days left before the premiere. The matter was again placed before the amiable ruler, although not without considerable reluctance. King Ernst was vastly amused at the singer's pompous presumption. "Let him have the horse," he laughed. "After all, what is a mere king compared with the Last of the Tribunes!"

Sure enough, Niemann took the king at his word. Every day for the next four the townspeople of Hanover were astonished to see a perfect stranger gravely acknowledging their almost automatic salutations from his perch high atop King Ernst's favorite white charger.

Above and beyond their obvious value, rehearsals often provide a useful outlet for tempers that might otherwise explode during performances. The best impresarios get pretty adept at handling such situations. During Metropolitan rehearsals of Mozart's *Don Giovanni* the memorable basso Ezio Pinza felt that he was being "sabotaged" by the man who was assigned the role of his servant Leporello. He may have been right: at any rate, the singer in question, Pavel Ludikar, used to sing the title role himself. True or not, the feeling so rankled Pinza that he finally announced that he was through. He was about to stalk away when Gatti-Casazza, who was seated onstage, shouted, "You stay right here and go on with the rehearsal!"

The surprised basso wheeled around and roared, "What are *you* doing on the stage? Go back to the office where you belong!"

Gatti went silently away, but Pinza did resume the rehearsal.

Handling rehearsal problems, of course, is only one portion, albeit a major one, of a manager's work of preparation for the Day of Judgment, the day when a production opens. He is, for example, faced with simple logistical difficulties occasioned by illness, accident, or what have you. The harried Colonel Mapleson was more prone to these hazards than most, probably because of his long lines of communication. One year he tried to run concurrent seasons on both sides of the Atlantic. He himself was headquartered in New York, and at one point he wired his London manager to send over immediately a "second tenor." The transoceanic request was misread so that Mapleson found himself accepting delivery on two tenors, one of whom had to be returned to England in a frantic rush in order to sing an Arturo in *Lucia di Lammermoor* for which he had already been announced.

The Colonel was nothing if not resourceful. At Her Majesty's Theatre he even got away with presenting a performance of *Il Trovatore* without a mezzo-soprano to sing the key role of the Gypsy woman Azucena. The artist hired for the part failed to show up, and Mapleson convinced the girl who sang the walk-on role of Inez to dress as Azucena and fake it. She didn't know more than a few notes of the role, but that didn't faze him at all. He cut the Second Act after the Anvil Chorus, brought her on to be condemned to the stake immediately in Act III, and instructed her to go silently to sleep, and stay that way, in Act IV. She was without question the most taciturn Gypsy ever seen on the operatic stage.

If shepherding people safely through an opening night can be harrowing, doing it for animals can seem downright lunatic. Most General Managers are faced with four-footed performers somewhere in their repertoire, but few have had to deal, as Gatti-Casazza once did at La Scala, with an elephant. It happened during 1901. On a double bill with a revival of Donizetti's *Linda di Chamounix* was scheduled to be an absurdly overblown ballet, *Amor*, which was fondly described by its modest creator Luigi Manzotti as a "great Choreographic Poem." In its two acts and sixteen scenes *Amor* purported to represent every significant event in the history of mankind from the Creation to the Battle of Legnano, where Barbarossa was defeated by the League of Italian Communes and the world was made safe for Latin culture. Manzotti wasn't joking, either: he actually intended compressing all the key moments of the past, as he understood them, into a monster pageant. The biggest of all the swollen scenes was to depict the triumphal entry of Julius Caesar into Rome, a significant event if ever Manzotti saw one, and for this he needed not only a veritable herd of horses but an ox and an elephant.

Already committed to this folly, Gatti-Casazza had little choice but to go along with the choreographer. So, he hired an accredited animal trainer and sent him to Hamburg, the nearest city that had an elephant for sale, to buy one. The deal was completed and the pachyderm, whose name was Papus, duly arrived in Milan by train. Gatti, who was a little nervous about the whole affair, almost panicked when he saw how large the beast actually was, but the trainer assured him that all would be well. He planned to lead Papus at night from the railroad station through the quiet streets of the city, when there would be less chance of encountering curious people and noisy conveyances. The procession began in docile enough fashion, with the elephant lumbering along equably behind the trainer, until suddenly Papus caught sight of a street car with a headlight on. The abrupt appearance of this odd one-eyed "beast" unnerved him completely. Despite the chains around his legs, and the sticks with hooks on the end manipulated by the trainer and his crew, Papus bolted. Gathering speed as he went, he charged down the street and right through a quiet *al fresco* dinner being enjoyed by a janitor and his family, resulting in a hue and cry that grew by leaps into a pandemonium. In practically no time a city-wide elephant hunt was in progress, right down to police and high-powered rifles. Papus, cornered and pretty winded, was just about to be shot when an equally-winded last-minute arrival by his trainer saved him; under the circumstances, there was nothing else to do but lead him glumly back to the railroad car.

By the next morning the Milan papers were full of the story. Papus and *Amor* became household words, and there was much attendant excitement when the elephant finally did arrive at La Scala, even though he was ignominiously delivered by van. Unfortunately, the trouble had not yet ended: no sooner had he entered the historic theatre than it was discovered that he was limping, apparently from a piece of glass imbedded in his heel sometime during his romp of the previous evening. As a lame elephant would hardly do for Caesar's entourage, immediate surgery was imperative. Papus was taken away to have an operation performed upon his foot.

By the time he returned to La Scala for rehearsals, wearing a large boot on his right rear leg, Papus was a very melancholy elephant. Things had not been going well. In order to cheer him up his trainer obtained the service of a small monkey named Pirri, who was an old friend. Pirri immediately set up light housekeeping on the pachyderm's back, to the evident delight of both animals. They got along famously; Papus snapped out of his blue funk, and rehearsals proceeded smoothly until the final dress. It was then that a palanquin complete with warrior was hoisted onto the elephant's back for the first time, an innovation he thoroughly resented. He snorted, took a sharp right turn and stampeded. Sets, dancers, extras, all were scattered by Papus' headlong rush, even a couple of little girls playing Cupids, who hid terrified under some scenery and weren't discovered until the next morning. He was finally brought to a halt, but not before La Scala had incurred a huge sum for the emergency repair of large numbers of breastplates, helmets and shields.

At last, in spite of all, *Amor* opened. What's more, it was a big hit, with not the least of its many attractions being Papus. A long run began. One night, though, chaos struck again. This time it was Papus' companion, Pirri the monkey, that was at the bottom of it all, or rather the top. He had somehow gotten loose just before the house was to be opened for the evening and began climbing all over the ceiling, jumping from box to box, generally having himself a high old time. Outside Scala the gathering audience was growing restive. Inside the tumult grew wilder as dozens of grown men clambered all over the auditorium trying to catch the elusive monkey. Finally, as Pirri sat high up in the gallery thumbing his nose at his pursuers, Gatti in desperation called for a shotgun, despite the damage that might result to his good relations with his star, Papus. Just as the bewhiskered Gatti had gotten his beard out of the sights and was about to fire, the trainer arrived, as always in the nick of time. He pushed the gun away and whistled. Pirri immediately leaped down from his vantage point and scrambled up to his trainer's shoulder, laughing, Gatti later maintained, in a squeaky voice. The doors were finally opened, the public calling "Down with the management" as they poured in.

The season finally ended, and with it the run of *Amor*. Gatti tried to sell Papus back to the people in Hamburg, but they claimed he was now damaged and worth only half-price, a figure Gatti was glad to accept. There is one final note to the story: the ox who had been Papus' co-star in the "great Choreographic Poem" was sold to a local Milanese butcher, who hung a sign in his window reading, "The Meat of the famous Ox of the Ballet *Amor* is sold here." Sic transit gloria mundi.

The necessity of keeping peace within his artistic family is forever pressing upon the impresario. Even ignoring the vicissitudes of performance and rehearsal, the daily problems that arise when you are trying to placate a company-full of willful individualists, some of them possessed of fairly odd notions, can be at best exasperating. Mapleson once estimated that during his engagement of the great American exponent and local creator of Carmen, Minnie Hauk, she would send him an average of between three and four notes of complaint per day. That's somewhat better than par for the course, but not unheard of, and managers learn to take this sort of thing in stride.

One of the greatest hazards of the trade seems to be the dressing room, assignment and decor of which often result in the wildest difficulty. Sir Thomas Beecham's first brush with Dame Nellie Melba, a moment likely to generate sparks under the best of circumstances, almost exploded under this kind of stress. It was the summer of 1919, and Beecham was presenting a special victory season at Covent Garden for which he had had the opera house spruced up a bit. Into his office stormed an infuriated Melba, wanting to know at the top of her expensive lungs why her room had been painted green. Sir Thomas, who had never worked with her before, decided quickly that the best defense is a good offense. Pretending not to recognize the celebrated diva, he demanded to know what precisely she meant by this unwarranted invasion of his privacy, particularly in so noisy a fashion, and even more particularly as he knew neither her nor of any private ownership of dressing rooms. Dame Nellie almost had a fit, but under his impassive and resolute silence she finally began to simmer down to the point where she declared that she would not have minded it so much if it were only a *cheerful* green. Beecham, who had been awaiting the opportunity, now made the grand gesture. He offered to have her room repainted. Melba was so delighted that she and Beecham became fast friends, proving again that timing is everything.

When Geraldine Farrar reigned at the Met she had a dressing room of her own, one not available for general use when she was not singing. This was a luxury denied her confrères before and since, although it should be noted that her underprivileged colleagues claimed the room was little more than a stuffy cubbyhole. What it did, of course, was keep Farrar from the possibility of ever getting embroiled in one of the recurrent dressing room feuds that every so often enliven the music pages. The most celebrated of these encounters, which became known in the press as "The Great Dressing Room Disturbance," took place near the end of the last century in Chicago.

The principals were Minnie Hauk and Marie Roze, with the harried Colonel Mapleson once more in the middle. The opera that night was to be Mozart's *The Marriage of Figaro* with Hauk as Cherubino and Roze as Susanna. As might have been expected, they both wanted the prima donna dressing room. At three o'clock in the afternoon Hauk arrived at the theatre and supervised the placing of her trunks and costumes therein. At four P.M. Roze's maid and husband arrived, removed Hauk's things and installed their own. At five-thirty Hauk's agent came by to check and discovered the switch. Once again the room was a scene of frenzied activity as he had Roze's effects tossed out and Hauk's returned, padlocking the place when he was done. Satisfied, he left, but the resourceful Marie Roze was not to be denied. She herself arrived at six, had a locksmith open the door, evicted Hauk's costumes, installed hers and got dressed. When Hauk came to the theatre a half-hour later, she saw *the* room occupied and returned immediately to her hotel, refusing to sing. Perforce the opera began without her, although, in a rather anticlimactic fashion, her lawyers persuaded her to appear by the beginning of Act II.

This preoccupation with accommodations does not stop with dressing rooms. Prima donnas have fought just as bitterly over hotel suites and railroad cars. In Dublin two Mapleson artists, the soprano Salla and the contralto Belocca, both demanded the "star" hotel suite. The impresario got the hotel manager to casually mention an "identical suite upstairs reserved for Lady Spencer," who was the wife of the Viceroy of Ireland. Belocca hinted around until she was shown the "reserved" suite, promptly claimed it for her own, and locked herself in, leaving Salla peacefully in possession of the disputed quarters.

Sometimes sending one prima donna upstairs can lead to trouble. Those were the arrangements that prevailed in a Boston hotel once, with Melba lodged directly below one of her arch-enemies, Lillian Nordica. The Australian diva sent a note to her rival that read in toto: "Since you are a New Englander, I suppose you *have* to have a rocking chair, but please don't rock so hard." Nordica would have been perfectly willing to oblige, except that she didn't have a rocking chair. It was finally determined that the noise Melba objected to was the maid's carpet sweeper.

Melba was not entirely wrong: noise above one's head can be horribly annoying. It even got to the generally easy-going Enrico Caruso when he was staying at a western hotel. His complaints to the proprietor brought the response that there was a wedding party lodged directly upstairs, but he would have Signor Caruso moved elsewhere immediately. "No," said the tenor. "Move the wedding party." And so it was.

During the great days of The Road, when touring opera companies traveled all over the world with the most scintillating rosters, a period that reached its zenith in the gracious half-century that ended with the First World War, impresarios were expected to supply their stars not only with sumptuous hotel space but with the most luxurious of railroad accommodations as well. For the front line prima donnas this meant lavishly appointed private cars whenever possible. Etelka Gerster, the brilliant coloratura who was Patti's big rival, often toured with the Mapleson Opera Company (sometimes along with Patti herself, an inflammable state of affairs, as we shall soon see). On one tour, the sleeping car in which she was traveling broke down and had to be side-tracked, but despite anguished pleas from Mapleson and assorted colleagues she refused to leave it and board another. *This* was the car she had picked out, and this was the one she wanted. No amount of logic could make her change her mind. She fully intended remaining in her car on its siding until it rusted away if need be. As we've already noted, Colonel Mapleson could be pretty inventive and tricky when necessary, and this was obviously one of those times. He abandoned the stubborn soprano to her solitude and retreated down the tracks to the station, where he had noticed that the station agent was an extraordinarily fine-looking man. A plot germinated. He persuaded the agent to dress up in some fancy clothes, then brought him back to Gerster's car and introduced him to the suspicious prima donna as the president of the railroad. The gentleman played his part admirably, softening her up with flattery, then begging her, in his capacity as head of this company, to do him the honor of using another car which he had specially put aside for her. Gerster, highly pleased at the attention of this captain of industry, finally allowed herself to be convinced. A carpet was laid from the door of the broken-down car to the new one, upon which she regally made her changeover on the arm of the station agent. The tour could continue.

It's hard to predict where the fancy of an opera singer might light to cause trouble for the impresario, calling upon all his resources and tact. A tenor named Mongini who was singing the Duke in *Rigoletto* for Mapleson threw a tantrum after Act III because the tailor had made his Act IV costume too tight. Not only did he refuse to go on, but he threatened anybody who came near him with his sword. The Colonel finally made himself heard over the imprecations, placating the raging tenor by assuring him that as soon as possible he would fire the offending tailor and make his family starve. Mongini finished the performance, tight pants and all. The next morning Mapleson (who had tipped off the tailor in advance) "fired" him in Mongini's presence. By now the tenor was over his pique of the previous night and was feeling sorry for the tailor's poor children. He begged the manager to reconsider and keep the man on the payroll, in return for which he would sing a performance for no fee. With a great show of reluctance, Mapleson agreed.

Incidentally, the tailor was a bachelor.

Not all of Mapleson's problems were so easily solved. His contract with Adelina Patti called for her name on all public announcements to be at least one-third larger than anyone else's, a prerogative she took quite literally. In Chicago one day Mapleson saw her husband, the tenor Nicolini, armed with a theodolite and accompanied by a gentleman who was apparently a professional geometrician, intently examining a large poster. Unsatisfied with his survey, Nicolini got a ladder and a ruler, climbed up and measured the letters directly. Horrors! Patti's name was *not* one-third larger than its nearest rival. It was merely an oversight, as Mapleson was quick to point out, but both husband and wife were furious. To mollify them, the Colonel had a thin slice removed from the next largest name, which happened to be that of the California-born soprano, Mlle. Emma Nevada (whose real name, by the way, was Wixom). The portion was excised from the middle of the name, so that the middle stroke of the letter "E" disappeared altogether. It looked a little peculiar, but at least it got within the size limits. Mapleson showed the revised version to Nicolini, who looked puzzled for a moment, then said, "all right, but there's something strange about that 'E'."

More direct, but more harrowing, was the curtain-time demand of a contralto who was to sing Ortrud in Houston for

Maurice Grau. She suddenly felt an overpowering necessity for certain plumbing facilities that were not available at the isolated theatre. She was quite certain she couldn't possibly go through *Lohengrin* in her condition: "No vessel, no performance" was her ultimatum. A trusted officer of the auditorium departed hastily for a desperate search around the neighborhood. His efforts finally proved fruitful, and he sneaked back into the theatre with the bulky but vital item hidden under his coat at what was reliably reported to be the eleventh hour.

Perhaps because of the highly-strung nervous system that seems to accompany vocal talent, singers have often tended to be an unreliable lot. Not dishonest or anything: it's just that some of them have been as likely to cancel as to appear. Managers have historically had their hands full making sure that the curtain goes up on a cast reasonably similar to the one that had been advertised. On one black day at New York's Academy of Music the opera was switched six times in the four hours before curtain time. First *William Tell* was changed to *Lucia,* which in turn was replaced by *Aida,* then *Rigoletto,* then *Les Huguenots* and then, ultimately, *La Favorita,* all as a result of cancellations.

The record for being most spectacularly left in the lurch probably belongs to Sir Thomas Beecham. For his 1911 season at Covent Garden he had determined to revive Tchaikowsky's *Pique Dame* and in an effort to make it as authentic-sounding as possible he had hired a beautiful and talented Eastern European soprano as his star on the recommendation of her embassy. Rehearsals proceeded admirably, so well in fact that everything was in perfect readiness a full three weeks before the scheduled premiere. The prima donna asked for and received permission from the pleased Sir Thomas to visit Paris for a few days, promising to return in ample time. She departed amid smiles and fond "au revoirs." Two of the three weeks went by with nary a word from Paris, until even the normally sanguine conductor-manager began to have his doubts. The day drew closer, and closer . . . and the soprano never returned. As a matter of fact, Beecham never heard from or saw her again. Even his inquiries through official channels were met with polite evasions, and for the rest of his life he never had the faintest idea of what had happened to her.

Beecham, of course, was a member of music's most privileged class, the conductors. To set an example, if nothing else, they are usually wherever they are supposed to be, and on time, but not always. They have used the weapon of the "sudden indisposition" as effectively as any prima donna. At the Metropolitan, for instance, the giant of them all, Arturo Toscanini, used this excuse to cancel a performance of *Tristan und Isolde* for which one of the principals had decided to skip rehearsals. *Götterdämmerung* was substituted with another conductor and the same leads.

Most of the time, though, the conductor is in the same boat with the impresario, dependent upon the caprice of the prima donna. At one time, "dependent" was hardly a descriptive enough word. Before Gatti-Casazza assumed the managerial reins at the Met it was customary for female artists to have a clause in their contracts guaranteeing them their fee even if they should fail to sing due to indisposition. The practical Gatti did away with the clause, and with the same stroke much of the "indisposition." It was the most effective cure-all since aspirin.

Many managers have relied upon demands for a doctor's certificate as proof of actual illness, but even this defense has often been meaningless. Minnie Hauk once walked out on Mapleson while his company was in Liverpool without so much as a moment's notice. Two days later a Doctor Weber sent a certificate claiming that Hauk was in precarious health, totally without voice, and desperately in need of some good resort air in Switzerland. It was December, and the good resort air was as likely to freeze her larynx as cure anything, but Mapleson had no choice other than to accept her departure with as good grace as he could muster. He later discovered that en route to Switzerland she had managed to gather enough strength to sing three solo recitals before, presumably, collapsing dramatically onto her profits.

Another Mapleson prima donna, Etelka Gerster, was on tour in St. Louis when she suddenly declared that she was unable to sing that evening's *Lucia*. She was informed that she would need a medical certificate, but the irascible soprano merely stuck her tongue out derisively at the physician and waltzed away. Unperturbed, the doctor wrote out a lengthy diagnosis based on his glimpse of her tongue claiming that she was suffering from "irritation in epiglottis, uvula contracted, throat muscles contracted and tonsils inflamed." Gerster's husband showed her the certificate, which so enraged her that she decided to sing after all just to prove that the doctor was an idiot. Idiot or no, he sent her a bill for sixty dollars for his professional services, which she refused to pay. The matter went into litigation, Gerster not being one to back away from a fight, and wasn't settled for two years. The court finally decided in her favor after a meeting in her hotel room at which she sang "The Last Rose of Summer" for the judge. Things have gotten less chummy nowadays.

Certificates *have* restored some fallen sopranos to grace. The celebrated coloratura Selma Kurz missed the Vienna premiere of Richard Strauss' masterpiece *Der Rosenkavalier* which was to have taken place on April 8th, 1911, with herself as Sophie. She had gotten into an altercation with the management because of a misunderstanding about the number of guests she might invite to the dress rehearsal and was summarily dropped from the cast. She regained her role for the second performance after humbly producing a medical report stating that the whole mess was due to a "nervous condition" brought on by the misunderstanding. Incidentally, when she did return the management had special guards posted all around the Staatsoper for fear that some of Kurz's innumerable partisans might make a disturbance. With that kind of popularity behind her, a doctor's certificate was obviously only a formality, if a useful one.

Matters didn't get as far as a certificate when, in 1882, Sofia Scalchi decided not to sing. It was in Philadelphia, and not until 5 P.M. did she remember to inform the long-suffering Colonel Mapleson that she didn't feel up to singing Amneris in *Aida* that night. He went charging up to her hotel room immediately with a doctor in tow, but skidded to a halt before knocking as he saw a waiter approaching with a laden dinner cart. Sure enough, the food—lobster salad and a roast duck—was for Scalchi. Mapleson and the physician waited until she had had sufficient time to get well started on her repast, then entered. Caught with the goods, so to speak, the contralto sang as scheduled.

Many a manager has sworn that the most capricious creature on the face of God's earth is not the soprano, but the tenor. A tenor has been defined as a singer with resonance where his brains ought to be; while this is hardly a fair generalization, it must be admitted that certain performers of the tenor persuasion have provided juicy evidence. One such was Signor Brignoli, who often appeared opposite Patti, Nilsson, and their great contemporaries. While singing in Havana one season he became displeased with what he felt was insufficient warmth on the part of the Cuban audience, deciding to punish them by working up a good sore throat and canceling his next performance. That, he figured, would show 'em. At the proper time he sent official notification to the management of the opera of his indisposition. What Brignoli didn't know was that under Cuban law any such sudden illness had to be reported to the government authorities, who promptly dispatched a public health physician to examine him. The doctor naturally found the singer to be in perfect health, so he gravely informed him that the diagnosis was acute yellow fever. Brignoli was so terrified he scooted to the opera house without another word and sang beautifully, simply to prove how free from disease he was.

A rival and sometime colleague of Brignoli was Luigi Ravelli, one of the few tenors *so* odd-ball as to confound even the quick-witted Mapleson. In New York he once informed the Colonel three-quarters of an hour before the theatre was to be opened that he wasn't well enough to sing Don Jose in that night's *Carmen*. Thoroughly used to this sort of thing, Mapleson took his accustomed direct action, hurrying to Ravelli's hotel room where he found the tenor looking fine but in bed, along with his pet dog Niagara. To Mapleson's demand that he get up immediately and stop making an idiot of himself, Ravelli replied crossly that he was tired and out of sorts. By an almost superhuman effort of the will, the impresario got him up and dressed and had him vocalize a little. The voice was in marvelous condition. Mapleson was about to haul the tenor off to the theatre when he insisted on consulting Niagara. The animal listened to his master sing, then growled, so Ravelli absolutely refused to appear. The Colonel had to cancel the performance.

Ravelli apparently played sick fairly often, usually on Mapleson's time. During a tour of Ireland in 1888 he became "ill" and stayed at a Dublin hotel for a week at Mapleson's expense. When the manager went to the hotel to notify him to prepare for a forthcoming concert, he demanded full pay for the week he was out malingering, or he would refuse to sing. This was more than Mapleson's strained nerves would bear: tempers rose until finally without warning Ravelli leaped at him, kicking out in all directions in what the Colonel later described as "the French style," while Signora Ravelli got in a few licks from the rear with a wooden chair. Almost as suddenly as it had begun the brawl stopped, everybody calmed down and, without the extra fees, the tenor sang as scheduled. It was worth, one hopes, a few black-and-blue marks.

Being an opera manager calls for not only quick thinking and the capacity to absorb punishment, but vast amounts of diplomacy, a word that in this context must include connotations of wiliness as well as tact. Michael Kelly, the tenor who gained lasting renown through his association with Mozart, was the stage manager of Goold's opera company in London when both the celebrated Mrs. Billington and her arch-rival Giuseppina Grassini were on the roster. The inevitable time came when Mrs. Billington was too sick to appear and the only possible substitute was Grassini, who naturally wasn't overjoyed at playing understudy. Her first reaction to the proposal was a scorching refusal, whereupon Mr. Kelly was sent around to her quarters on the morning of the performance to try his luck. He informed her that he had come merely to say that he approved wholeheartedly of her firm stand; after all, he was a performer himself and understood these things. Grassini was delighted, and the interview was terminated on a note of mutual cordiality. As he was about to leave, Kelly suddenly turned and said, "By the bye, it's a pity you won't be on tonight: the Lord Chamberlain's office has just apprised us that Queen Charlotte was coming incognito, with the princesses, just to hear you, but don't you worry, I'll tell the Lord Chamberlain and express your regrets."

Before Kelly was half-way through his speech, Grassini had changed her mind. She didn't discover that it was all a fib until she was well into the evening's opera, *La Vergine del Sole*, by which time she was in a fine mood and willing to laugh at her own gullibility, which was more than most prima donnas have ever been willing to do.

Probably the most unreliable singer of all time was Catarina Gabrielli. During the height of her career she would cancel appearances whenever the mood was upon her, a fairly common occurrence. The only way to convince her to sing would be to get her current lover to sit conspicuously in front of the pit or in a stage box. If Gabrielli hadn't quarreled with him recently—an ever-present likelihood—and if she hadn't grown tired of him, she would forget her malaise and go out on stage. She would warble directly at her favorite, of course, all through the performance, but at least the manager didn't have to refund any admission fees. Effective as this gambit was for a while, even La Gabrielli got suspicious after a few times, so that it succeeded less and less often. It would have come in handy during her brief stay in England. By the time she arrived there her powers were probably on the wane; whatever the reason she was greeted by English audiences with a great deal less than the enthusiasm to which she had become accustomed on the Continent. She exacted her revenge for this coolness by singing in a careless, sloppy manner whenever she chose to sing at all, which wasn't particularly often. She preferred to remain sick on even the most important occasions, frequently sending her not-very-talented sister Francesca to sing for her. Her engagement ended not long after the manager of the company came to her apartment to inquire after her apparently failing health and found a tremendous party in progress—to which, compounding the injury, he hadn't even been invited.

Not all instances of undependability can be traced to pure whim; enlightened self-interest has also prompted prima donna walk-outs. The chain of events that led to Melba's sensational debut in Brussels, with its resultant world-wide attention, involved a broken contract. She had been studying for some time in Paris with the great vocal teacher Madame Mathilde Marchesi (who also taught Calvé, Gerster, Emma Eames and Frances Alda, among others) when Maurice Strakosch, the impresario, heard her vocalizing and signed her on the spot to an exclusive contract calling for 1,000 francs a month for the first year, 2,000 for the next, and so on. To young Nellie, this seemed the height of opulence. Shortly afterwards, however, Marchesi's studio again was visited, this time by Messrs. Dupont and Lapissida, the directors of Brussels' famed Theatre de la Monnaie. They heard a fresh young voice tossing off a few roulades in another room, demanded to be introduced to this phenomenon—Melba, naturally—and offered her a contract calling for an immediate debut, 3,000 francs a month, and all her own costumes to keep. The flabbergasted soprano stammered out a few hesitant objections about her previous commitment to Strakosch, but Marchesi, claiming to be a dear personal friend of the impresario, convinced Melba that she would take care of the whole thing. Nellie signed with Brussels.

She was about to leave Paris about a week later to fulfill her engagement when Strakosch burst into her flat, almost apoplectic with rage, demanding to know if these vicious rumors about her going to the Theatre de la Monnaie were true. Melba, who hadn't bothered to inform him about the change in her plans, admitted it but claimed that Marchesi had assured her that she would take care of everything. This intelligence sent him off into another burst of fury that culminated in screaming denunciations as he stormed off. Melba, shaken but determined, and also unwilling to face *that* sort of thing again, departed immediately for Brussels.

She was greeted warmly, but as rehearsals were about to begin a troop of gendarmes arrived armed with a court order forbidding her to appear at La Monnaie. Lapissida tried everything he could, but to no avail. Strakosch was adamant and he had the law on his side. It appeared that little Nellie's career was over before it had begun. She moped around Brussels brooding about her sins as the day of the scheduled debut drew closer, the future looking bleak indeed, until fate took a hand. Lapissida came charging over to her one day, all out of breath, and gasped out the news: Strakosch had dropped dead. The tidings had just been flashed to them. Melba, thus freed from her contract, sang Gilda in *Rigoletto* on October 13, 1887, at the Theatre de la Monnaie in Brussels, quite literally over the dead body of an impresario.

It is not inevitable, however, that the impresario come out the loser. One of the most difficult artists in operatic history was certainly Victor Maurel. An excellent actor and effective vocalist, he was also arrogant, impertinent, tardy, willful, cruel, vain and untrustworthy, a sort of upside-down Boy Scout. At least, this was the way he seemed to the harried managers under whose banners he performed. Typical is the time he refused to sing *Rigoletto* in Philadelphia because he didn't like the soprano who was scheduled to replace the indisposed Melba, a girl named Marie van Cauteren. The embarrassed impresario told the already assembled audience that he would have to cancel the performance because Maurel's costumes hadn't arrived. This sort of behavior characterized his every move during one three-month season at La Scala that was run by a manager named Corti. Corti kept his peace while the season was on, no matter how vile Maurel's actions, but on the day the schedule ended he called the baritone to his office, said "good day," and asked him to be seated on the sofa. No sooner had Maurel sat down than Corti, who was small but wiry, grabbed him by the neck and pushed him backwards until the astonished singer was lying prone, then began punching away at his head. The fusillade continued until Corti was winded. "Now," he said, "I am satisfied," and he shoved Maurel to the door. The stunned singer left quietly. As the door was closing, Corti cried triumphantly after him, "Now, dear Maurel, we are even!"

And so they were.

Chapter 3

The Hatfields and the McCoys

IF SINGERS create problems for managers, it's nothing to the problems they create for each other. No profession on earth has generated nearly so many vitriolic feuds, nor ones so fascinating to watch, as has opera. The recent Tebaldi-Callas fracas was largely fluff compared with some of the wingdingers that have happened in the past, but it was enough fun to command headline space, and stories in *Time*. A peculiar gusto marks operatic rivalries, making them at once more intense and vastly more amusing than, say, a battle between members of the board of A. T. & T. They arise from a wide variety of causes: simple jealousy, overlapping repertoire, personal dislike, sometimes even an instinct for self-preservation. One of the most well-known opera stories, and perhaps a true one, is about the baritone who was being unmercifully hissed by the hard-to-please fans in Parma, notoriously the most difficult audience in Italy. He took it as long as he could, then stopped singing and held up his hands for silence. As soon as he could make himself heard, he said, "If you think I'm bad, wait until you hear the tenor!"

The earliest documented prima donna feud of any magnitude was carried on by two of Handel's sopranos, Faustina Bordoni and Francesca Cuzzoni. The composer had imported Cuzzoni first, some years before the pretty Bordoni. Cuzzoni was tremendously gifted, but just as tremendously hard to handle. Handel put up with her tantrums, her whims, and her homely visage for a long time because of her talent, even writing special songs for her, but she became ever more difficult. At one point, when she obstinately refused to sing a new aria Handel had composed, he grabbed her by the scruff of the neck and dangled her out a window, threatening to let go unless she changed her mind. She sang the aria.

Obviously, threats of defenestration form an unstable basis for continuing harmonious dealings, so Handel imported the sweet-tempered Bordoni, whom Cuzzoni detested on sight. Faustina would have been just as glad to get along nicely with everybody, but her older rival kept the fight simmering constantly, getting nastier at every attempt at conciliation and really baring her fangs when Bordoni showed her pretty face anywhere near. In short order London society was divided into two opposing camps, each championing one of the singers, and Bordoni was swept willy-nilly along. The whole affair became the biggest news item of the day.

It reached its climax during the month of June, 1727, when both mezzo-sopranos appeared in the same performance of Bononcini's *Astianatte*. The theatre was jammed with a brilliant crowd, including royalty and the leaders of English society, with both factions primed for the event. No sooner had the two prima donnas appeared than the audience broke into a cacophonic storm of mingled hisses and cheers, catcalls and applause, that continued despite the presence of royalty and the best efforts of the management. The uproar so infected the artists involved that they forgot their manners as completely as had the ladies in the stalls, even, according to reports, coming to blows. The biggest ruckus was stirred up by Pembroke's party, on Cuzzoni's side, which prompted a contemporary wag to have the following epigram circulated the next day:

> Old poets sing that beasts did dance
> Whenever Orpheus played;
> So to Faustina's charming voice
> Wise Pembroke's asses brayed.

The continuing contention, what with singers bashing each other around, was soon made the subject of a popular farce that ran with great success at Heidigger's Theatre in London. Called *Contretemps, or the Rival Queens*, it depicted Bordoni as the Queen of Bologna and Cuzzoni as the Princess of Modena, both addicted to pulling hair and scratching faces. As they are hard at each other, Handel cynically looks on and orders that they be "left to fight it out, inasmuch as the only way to calm their fury is to let them satisfy it."

Actually, the directors of the opera finally found a more expedient solution. As it became increasingly evident that the situation was tending toward chaos, the decision was reached to get rid of one of the two rivals. Bordoni was both the more attractive and easily the more tractable, so it was Cuzzoni that would have to go. Because she could not be summarily dismissed without running the risk of plunging England into another Civil War, a more subtle means had to be uncovered. Fortunately for the stability of the London musical scene, Cuzzoni herself provided the out. Someone remembered that she had solemnly sworn never to accept a guinea less than was paid Bordoni; accordingly, Bordoni was immediately offered precisely one guinea more than Cuzzoni was making. Cuzzoni heard about it via a well-planned leak, broke her contract angrily and sailed for Vienna. The first of the great feuds thus came to an end.

Rivalry must be accepted as one of the hazards of doing business when you are rash enough to include on your roster two prima donnas of the same voice-category with cherished reputations to protect. Unfortunately, almost every company with pretensions to international significance must necessarily do precisely that, and more. Seldom, though, has any impresario been faced with the daily inflammability that was Colonel Mapleson's lot during the time he toured America with both Etelka Gerster and Adelina Patti in his company. Both were brilliant coloraturas with excursions into more dramatic territory, both commanded tremendous popularity, both were world-famed, both were volatile, and both were just the littlest bit wacky. It made for a fairly gothic trip around the country.

Although there was a marked antipathy between the two stars from the moment they met, the actual beginning of their open warfare might be said to date from a performance of Meyerbeer's *Les Huguenots* that Mapleson presented in Chicago. Gerster sang the Queen and Patti was Valentine. Although she appears in Act I, Valentine doesn't have much to do until later, while the Queen's part in Act I is full of spectacular vocal folderol. Nevertheless, when the First Act curtain calls were taken a flock of ushers filed to the footlights laden with flowers, all destined for Patti. Bouquet after huge bouquet were handed up to her as the audience began losing its patience, until finally, in the middle of all this floral opulence, one humble little basket of posies was handed up to Gerster. The crowd cheered wildly, much to Patti's helpless rage, and the performance continued in an atmosphere of ill-concealed hostility. When she finally got back to her hotel room, Adelina kicked and screamed on the floor until she was forcibly put to bed, still crying out terrible vows about never again singing in the same opera with that woman Gerster.

It got to the point where Patti began believing that Gerster had the evil eye. This may seem like nonsense in the day of the televised news-conference, but many an opera star would swear otherwise. Patti's husband, the tenor Nicolini, agreed wholeheartedly with his wife's analysis of the situation, and between the two of them Gerster's "evil eye" became the focal point of blame for any misfortune that might befall them, great or small. During a San Francisco earthquake when the ground began to shake beneath Patti's feet, she was heard to mutter "Gerster!"

So firmly was this whole business planted in Patti's mind that whenever her rival's name was mentioned or her presence suggested she would extend the first and fourth fingers of her right hand in the horn sign that was supposed to avert the evil eye's malevolent effects. Once, both prima donnas were lodged at the same hotel. As Patti was walking down a dark hallway past Gerster's room on the way to her own, she jabbed out her two fingers and almost poked the eyes out of

Dr. Gardini, Gerster's husband, who at that very instant had opened his door to put his shoes in the hall before going to bed.

During the height of the feud, in the 1880's, it became known that General Crittenden, the Governor of Missouri, had publicly kissed Patti. The incident became something of a cause célèbre, which Adelina described thusly:

"I had just finished singing 'Home, Sweet Home' when a nice-looking old gentleman, who introduced himself as Governor Crittenden, began congratulating me. All of a sudden he leaned down, put his arms around me, drew me up to him, and kissed me. He said, 'Madame Patti, I may never see you again, but I cannot help it'; and before I knew it he was kissing me. When a gentleman, and such a nice old gentleman, too, and a Governor of a great state, kisses one so quick that one has not time to see and no time to object, what can one do?"

Shortly afterwards, the following interview with Gerster was published under the headline, "That Patti Kiss":

"Modest Reporter: 'I suppose, Madame Gerster, you have heard about that kissing affair between Governor Crittenden and Patti?'

Madame Gerster: 'I have heard that Governor Crittenden kissed Patti before she had time to resist, but I don't see anything in that to create so much fuss.'

Reporter: 'You don't?'

Gerster: 'Certainly not! There is nothing wrong in a man kissing a woman old enough to be his mother.' "

One or the other of his two stars was forever walking out on Colonel Mapleson, usually without notice, and almost always in a rage over the other one. Thus, Gerster took the first train back to New York from Baltimore when she discovered her name on a playbill in smaller type than Patti's and tickets for her performances selling for lower prices. Mapleson himself had to go and retrieve her personally. For all the trouble they caused when they were together, the prima donnas did serve as a kind of check-and-balance on each other, which the manager found very useful and worth preserving, even at the price of becoming a kind of fancy referee. Every time one of them bolted, the one left behind, freed of restraint, would become impossibly capricious. A trip to New York was a small sacrifice under the circumstances.

This delicate equilibrium was never more apparent to Mapleson than the time in St. Louis when it seemed that Patti had left the company. Gerster, feeling liberated from the pressures of competition, reverted to type. She became hopelessly hard to manage. On the day the troupe was to depart from St. Louis for the West she suddenly refused to leave, went to bed, and ordered her maid to unpack her dresses and hang them in the closet. While she fiddled around her hotel room, Mapleson's special train waited at the station. After an extremely uncomfortable period, Patti heard about Gerster's intractability. Summoning her maid immediately, she sent word to Mapleson that she would again sing for him, regardless of their differences, rather than leave him at the mercy of such a one as Gerster. At almost the same precise moment *Gerster* had a change of heart, both prima donnas arriving at the station with their retinues just about simultaneously. From *no* leading sopranos, Mapleson had gone back to his normal quota of quarreling. Things simmered close to the boiling point until Denver, where Gerster saw Patti announced for a performance of *La Traviata*, which she deemed her rightful property. Without a word, she left the hotel, went to the station, and ordered a special train at Mapleson's expense to take her back to New York en route to Europe. Patti was now in sole command, and nobody was allowed to forget it.

The multiplicity of causes for rivalry is a wonder to behold —Marie Van Zandt and Emma Nevada feuded simply because they were both born in the Western United States—but the factor that keeps them going once begun is more often than not the active partisanship of the public. In the case of these two American artists, when Van Zandt got sick during a performance her adherents made a concerted effort to convince the authorities and anyone else who would listen that

Nevada had arranged to have their favorite drugged. In this kind of atmosphere truce-making is hardly feasible.

Some of the most surprising people get involved in long-term battles. Emma Eames always gave the impression of being somehow above it all, but in her way she fought with the best of them. Marcella Sembrich was the object of her disfavor for some time, and not even a natural catastrophe could smooth it over. They were both caught in the San Francisco earthquake, and Eames, who was staying with some friends, invited her colleagues Andreas Dippel, Pol Plançon and Sembrich to join her on grounds that were somewhat safer than the St. Francis Hotel, maintaining her frigid silence towards the Polish soprano throughout the entire episode.

It was Eames, too, who described Frances Alda to the Duchess de Richelieu as "all right for the chorus."

The major feud of Eames' life, though, was carried on vigorously with the volcanic Emma Calvé. This one often had opportunity for public display as they occasionally sang Micaëla and Carmen in the same performances of *Carmen*, especially during the Metropolitan season of 1893–94. Whenever they did, tempers were under stress from the moment the cast was announced; by the closing curtain only professional dignity prevented mayhem. At one curtain call in Chicago Calvé snatched her hand away from Eames during the bow, scattering combs and scarves all over the stage. Fernando de Lucia, the evening's Don Jose, gallantly bent to retrieve some of the fallen debris, but was withered by a Calvé glance and fled the stage, dragging a scarf behind him.

Nellie Melba, a colleague of both women but a friend of Calvé, when asked in 1894 if the quarrel was still on, said in her coldest tones, "I have no idea. I do not know Madame Eames."

By all odds the least likely candidates for a feud might easily have been Lotte Lehmann and Elisabeth Schumann, two of the most gracious sopranos ever to enhance the stage, and ultimately very dear comrades; yet early in their careers they became embroiled by inevitable jealousies. After her first big success at Hamburg, as Anna in Nicolai's *The Merry Wives of Windsor,* Lehmann was promised Sophie in the forthcoming local premiere of Strauss' *Der Rosenkavalier.* The young soprano, astonished and overjoyed, applied herself zealously to studying the role. She was therefore all the more bitterly disappointed when the opening Sophie was taken from her and given to Elisabeth Schumann at the request of Edyth Walker, the Octavian, because of Schumann's slightly greater experience. Schumann was, of course, radiantly lovely in the role, but Lehmann was convinced that it was all a plot. She cast Schumann in her own mind as, to quote her, the "world's greatest intriguer—a role which, heaven knows, was quite foreign to her nature." She herself was put-upon and misunderstood, she felt, and she bitterly resented the idea of being in the second cast. Schumann went to great lengths to be nice, but Lehmann wasn't buying any, thank you. She had a good mad worked up, and if she wanted to loathe Schumann, nothing was going to stop her. She had once been told something that she now was beginning to believe: all colleagues are your enemies.

Fortunately for those who have faith in humanity, Lehmann soon got over her pique and remained, despite later provocations from certain glamorous rivals, one of the most considerate and amiable of stars. She shortly deserted the role of Sophie for that of the Marschallin in *Der Rosenkavalier,* and before long the dream cast, containing both Lehmann *and* Schumann, was a reality.

This same bugaboo, competition for a role, gave birth to one of the most delightful stories to come out of the Metropolitan in some years. A few seasons ago the brilliant American soprano Eleanor Steber sang a broadcast matinee of Puccini's *Tosca* that was exceptionally beautiful. At the end, however, when Tosca jumps off the parapet atop the Castel Sant' Angelo, Miss Steber discovered too late that the mattress upon which Met Toscas are supposed to land was slightly out of position. She avoided serious injury, but the off-balance fall broke one of her teeth. The audience, knowing nothing

of this, kept calling her back for enraptured curtain calls as
the afternoon ended on a triumphant note.

That evening the leading lady was a prima donna, one of
whose roles happened also to be Tosca. As she was preparing
for her first entrance a backstage assistant, making small talk
with her in the wings, said, "By the way, I understand Miss
Steber broke a tooth this afternoon."

The soprano flashed a knowing smile. "I told her she should
not sing Tosca: it is too heavy for her!"

Olive Fremstad and Johanna Gadski, competing for status
as the Met's first-line Wagnerian soprano during the first
decades of this century, engaged in an intramural struggle
that manifested itself publicly, like the Eames-Calvé ruckus,
mostly during curtain calls. While the majority of works call
for only one leading soprano, many Wagnerian music-dramas
call for two (such as *Die Walküre* and *Tannhäuser*, for example) so that they often had occasion to appear together. On
one such evening each arranged with her fans to cram the
stage with flowers, neither being aware of the other's intent.
As a result, at the final bows both sopranos were practically
buried under huge mounds of horticulture. Gadski, a strapping
woman, fought her way through the towering foliage back to
the footlights but Fremstad found herself driven completely
offstage by the onslaught of roses. Floral offerings were held
to a minimum thereafter, but the struggle continued. At one
Walküre Gadski, playing Brünnhilde, deliberately scratched
the arm of Fremstad (Sieglinde) near the end of Act II. As
they held hands at the curtain call, the Divine Olive pur-
posely allowed the blood to drip onto Gadski's costume, holding her still so that the audience could see.

Curtain calls have traditionally provided a point of conflict.
In 1950 the Metropolitan revived Johann Strauss' *Fledermaus*
with tremendous success. In the cast were such luminaries as
the American mezzo-soprano Risë Stevens as Orlofsky and
the sensational Ljuba Welitch as Rosalinda, both of them old
hands at stage tricks. Welitch, though, was not as familiar
with the topography of the Met as was Stevens: when they
came out for their bows she gravitated naturally to center

stage, but Stevens, playing the part of the gallant confrère, whispered to her that she was too far left, that she had better move a little to the right in order to get center stage. Welitch complied, which placed her far to the audience left and brought the beaming Risë smack-dab to the middle where she felt she belonged. It was a neat ploy, but there's no record of how long it remained effective.

To a certain extent an artist's response to the lure of the curtain call can be read as providing a clue to his or her total personality. While it doesn't replace Freud, the method is illuminating. Thus, when the gentle but scintillating coloratura Amelita Galli-Curci was urged by a tenor to take a solo bow so he could do likewise and reap the full benefit of his claque, she replied, "No, thank you. I make my reputation while the curtain is up, not while it is down."

On the other hand, when Melba sang for the first time with John McCormack at Covent Garden and he started to take a bow, it is said she haughtily reminded him that "in this house *nobody* takes bows with Melba."

Melba, incidentally, was never one to waste words. When she heard Campanini had engaged Frances Alda for New York she promptly wired, "EITHER ALDA OR MYSELF." Alda later claimed that she was delighted to have her contract broken, as she went directly on to La Scala, Gatti-Casazza and what have you. Sometimes, Melba would wither her competition without the necessity of even so brief a message, taking refuge instead in direct action, as in the Covent Garden performance of *La Bohème* in which Fritzi Scheff scored a brilliant personal success as Musetta. Melba simply refused to proceed past Act II of *Bohème* despite the best efforts of the management. She finished the evening singing the Mad Scene from *Lucia di Lammermoor*.

Come to think of it, Melba managed to feud with almost every prima donna who posed the slightest threat to her cherished feeling of supremacy, including some of the least likely. Lillian Nordica, for example, sang precious few roles that Dame Nellie would ever in her right mind want to include in her own repertoire, but Melba feuded nonetheless.

Until her disastrous brush with Brünnhilde, she had visions of herself as the "complete" prima donna doing Lucia one night and Isolde the next; at any rate, she coveted Nordica's roles, had sung some of them, and envied her status, and the feeling was probably mutual. Between them, they gave Maurice Grau, then managing the Metropolitan, a difficult time. He assigned each of them two opening nights in a kind of desperate "share-the-wealth" policy which didn't alleviate matters much. Melba, on one of her opening nights, saw Nordica sitting in the front row and told Grau she wouldn't go on unless her rival were ejected. Grau refused to do any such thing, claiming that as a purchaser of a ticket Nordica had every right to sit wherever she pleased. Dame Nellie of course sang. Nobody remembers now whether or not Nordica applauded.

The relationship of Melba to most of the rest of the operatic world can perhaps be summarized by her comment after she and Mary Garden had sung together at Windsor Castle during a state dinner for the King of Greece. "What a dreadful concert this would have been if I hadn't come," she told the court chamberlain.

Garden, not one to be dismayed by bitchery, brushed aside attempts to cover Melba's remark. "Please don't bother about me, Lord Farquhar," she said. "I love Melba's rudeness. It amuses me."

By this time in her career Garden had become accustomed to impoliteness, as most stars must. It was she who was the butt of Calvé's remarks when the two of them, along with some colleagues, were taking a late supper at the Savoy after a Covent Garden performance. She was wearing a perfume created especially for her. Calvé sniffed the air, then demanded to have her table changed. "I shall not be able to eat," she said, "or I shall be sick."

The Scotch soprano learned soon enough to take care of herself. By the time her career had reached its zenith she was the most accomplished scene-stealer in the business. Some of her contemporaries even accused her of employing four-legged confederates. There is no question but that the donkey she used in one of her greatest successes (Massenet's *Le Jongleur de Notre Dame*, first revived for her by Hammerstein at the Manhattan Opera House in 1908) invariably pricked up its ears when she sang and looked despondent whenever anybody else did. He may simply have been a fan, of course, but a certain amount of pre-curtain encouragement was suspected. There was a segment of the audience that would come just to see the donkey do his stuff, and he never failed.

Garden's reputation as a good in-fighter probably dates from her very first major victory, being assigned Mélisande in the world premiere of Debussy's operatic masterpiece *Pelléas et Mélisande*. It had been verbally agreed between Debussy and the writer of the play, Maurice Maeterlinck, that the role would go to Maeterlinck's common-law wife, Georgette Le Blanc, but Garden, who was a *particular* friend of André Messager and much admired by Albert Carré, the Director of l'Opéra-Comique, got the nod. Maeterlinck fought hard to no avail, and there is no doubt that his continuing dislike for Debussy and for the opera started with this rebuff. He even threatened to beat up the composer, seriously contemplated challenging him to a duel, and became an open enemy of everybody involved with *Pelléas et Mélisande*. He wrote a letter to the Paris newspaper *Le Figaro* before the premiere that contained a vivid denunciation of the management of the Opéra-Comique as well as a fervent wish for "the immediate and emphatic failure" of the opera. He may even have been responsible for the writing and distribution of a vicious parody of the play which was distributed outside the theatre just before dress rehearsal. In short, because of Garden's prowess when the chips were down, he did everything in his power to demean the work he was so responsible for creating. That he failed in this attempt reflects the greater credit on the artistry of all concerned, including himself.

This same role was the hub of another squabble not very long after this time, at the same theatre. In 1908, by which time Garden was the darling of New York, a young soprano named Maggie Teyte was suddenly dismissed from her position at the Opéra-Comique by the (still) director Albert Carré, only to find herself just as suddenly rehired a few days

later. To cap her confusion, the role she was assigned was—
plum of all plums—Mélisande, which she had been studying
with Debussy himself. Teyte, almost beside herself with surprise and delight, applied herself diligently throughout the
three-month-long rehearsal period to the task of becoming
Garden's successor. It was only then that she discovered the
real reason behind M. Carré's abrupt change of heart. He
apparently wanted *Pelléas et Mélisande* back in his company's repertoire because it had been such a hit with Garden
starring, and it was rumored around Paris that Garden herself might return to do the role. This possibility was entirely
too much for Carré's jealous wife Marguerite, who was
incidentally a soprano, so she pushed Teyte for the job until
such time as she herself could learn the part. Carré went
along, and so did Teyte even after she learned the facts, at
least until she had scored a fine success in the role. She then
seized the first opportunity that presented itself (it happened
to be a contract with Beecham's company at His Majesty's
Theatre in London) to leave the Opéra-Comique gracefully
before Marguerite Carré could have her sacked. Madame
Carré immediately took over as Mélisande.

This sort of finagling is not the exclusive property of the
Latin temperament, by any means. Two distinctively American products were involved at the Metropolitan during the
1937–38 season. One was the late Lawrence Tibbett, then the
undisputed reigning king of the baritones. The other was a
young man with a gorgeous voice, the young (and now also
"the late") Leonard Warren. Warren had been assigned the
role of Ford in Verdi's *Falstaff* in which Tibbett was to do
the title role, singing it at all the rehearsals. At the performance, though, Ford was sung by John Brownlee. There can
never be any proof, but the assumption has always been that
Tibbett remembered how, as Ford, he had himself once stolen
the show from Antonio Scotti's Falstaff and was taking no
chances on history repeating itself. It's not unlikely.

For all the force of backstage machinations, the fights that
are the most fun for us, the paying public, are naturally the
ones that take place in full view during the course of an

opera. It's always seemed a pity that the on-stage duel (for real) between Franco Corelli and Boris Christoff that boiled up a few seasons ago over relative stage placement did so at a dress rehearsal rather than a regularly scheduled performance. That would have been a doozy to see. It was in a grand tradition, too, a tradition replete with episodes at least as remarkable as sword-play.

Some of the incidents have been small, but none the less embarrassing. When David Bispham, the American baritone, used to sing Iago to the Otello of Tamagno he would put his foot on the body of the prostrate Moor as he said the line "Ecco il leone"; it was an effective piece of business, to which the creator of the role of Otello had no objection whatsoever. In 1901, however, Bispham found himself opposite Albert Alvarez in an *Otello* that had seen the usual minimum of rehearsal. The cue came for Iago to derisively point to the fallen "lion" and Bispham, as was his wont, put his foot on Otello's chest. Alvarez, taken unawares, hated the whole thing. The audience was treated to the unsettling spectacle of a supposedly unconscious tenor reaching up and shoving the offending foot forcibly away. The baritone attached to the foot almost plunged headlong alongside his prone but active adversary, managing to regain his balance only just in time to prevent an amusing scene from becoming a completely uproarious fiasco. It is presumed that thenceforward Bispham took pains to see that the Otellos he performed with were either forewarned or actually unconscious.

Tamagno, despite his high repute and a self-confidence that easily allowed him to suffer Bispham's foot, always traveled with a personal eight-man claque for whom seats at each performance were guaranteed by contract. It was an unnecessary precaution. Not only was he good, he was *loud*. His voice was of such overwhelming size that even had he been a less effective singer than he was, audiences would have been clobbered into enthusiasm by the sheer volume. This legendary lung-power made for certain difficulties with his contemporaries, though. Not many sopranos could make themselves heard in duets once he got wound up. Luisa Tetrazzini, of all people, was one of the many who found themselves on the losing side, and yet she was denied even recourse to resentment because Tamagno was singing with her as a favor in the first place. It was in South America, where the coloratura was to make her debut as Lucia di Lammermoor, a big event indeed, except that as it became more imminent it was realized that no proper tenor was available. Tamagno volunteered to do Edgardo as a favor to his friend Luisa, answering the shocked disbelief evident around him with a promise to scale his voice down to the lyric requirements of both the part and his leading lady. He tried, too, for a few bars, but under the stimulus of performance he soon forgot, merrily blasting away at the top of his awesome voice by the time the first-act love duet was fairly under way. Tetrazzini, certain she had been completely drowned out, sidled over to the tenor and whispered, "Do hold in your voice, Tamagno, or no one will ever hear me." It did no good. He smiled, cautioned her to take a good deep breath, and roared his way through the rest of the opera with such gusto that the stage floor actually trembled from the vibrations. Both artists were acclaimed mightily by the audience at the end of the evening, but Tetrazzini remained certain that, deafened as they were by Tamagno, they hadn't heard a note she had sung.

For some reason, most of the memorable on-stage squabbles seem to be mixed-singles affairs, usually involving as classic opponents a tenor and a soprano. As a rule they are both active participants, although the first big fight Lilli Lehmann ever was involved in began with her as a completely innocent bystander. It was in an 1870 Berlin performance of *Rienzi* starring the mighty Albert Niemann as the Last of the Tribunes, a role that always went to his head anyway. Rienzi's big scene on this occasion was quite ruined by the actions of two half-blind comprimarios and Marianne Brandt. They played, respectively, a pair of conspirators and Adriano, lover of Rienzi's sister Irene (Lilli Lehmann this night). For some reason, the two myopic bit-players stayed on stage in full view as Niemann's big scene progressed, and Brandt perforce remained with them. To their foggy vision the frantic gestures of Rienzi and the supposedly unconscious Irene for them to go back seemed like an invitation to take a greater part in the proceedings, so they came stage-center and mugged away conspiratorially at the audience. The climax of Niemann's performance was wrecked. His fury at the whole affair engulfed the nearest victim it could find, which happened to be Lehmann, who had had nothing to do with it. The three miscreants vanished as soon as the curtain fell, but the tenor grabbed Lehmann's arm in a grip of steel, forcing her to take all his curtain calls with him. He started to drag her off in search of his tormentors, but when she tried to intercede on their behalf, he turned upon her and singed her ears with invective for a few choice minutes. She finally broke away, running to her room in tears. She didn't speak to Niemann for three years, in spite of their close working proximity, although later they became close friends. Brandt and her near-sighted buddies apparently got off scot-free.

Wagnerian music-dramas seldom allow much room for individual bickering, with a few exceptions like *Rienzi*. For one thing, the mystique that still surrounds them tends to dampen the normally exuberant and combative prima donna nature. For another, they are usually carefully staged, with slow and deliberate pageant-like actions effectively preventing the improvisation that is the heart of good "up-staging" contests. Lastly, for long stretches people sing either alone or to one other person who remains stock-still a hundred feet away, both of them seemingly in a deep trance. Little of this, incidentally, is Wagner's doing: it's a carry-over from the deadly turn-of-the-Century days when Wagner was the only true god and Cosima was his prophetess. In spite of it all, the antic spirit has occasionally reared its head. Helen Traubel, for one, became involved in minor disputes with some of her tenors. As Brünnhilde in *Siegfried* she once hid the diminutive but talented Set Svanholm completely behind the billowing negligee designed for her by Adrian of Hollywood. As he vanished from sight he cannot be said to have presented a particularly heroic appearance. Traubel kept her draperies more firmly under control at subsequent performances.

Traubel's one continuing battle, and a friendly one at that, was with the marvelous Danish heldentenor Lauritz Melchior, with whom she often sang. He once told her, shortly after she made her impressive Wagnerian debut at the Metropolitan (she had sung there briefly two years before in Damrosch's *Man Without a Country*), that the most important thing was always to give every note its precise value. He then proceeded to hold every climactic note as long as he could. As soon as she caught on, she did exactly the same thing, and the game continued every time they appeared together. She did pretty well for herself, but later admitted that in direct competition Melchior would always hold his note longer: he seemed to enjoy turning purple.

More fertile than Wagner as a field for on-stage scuffling is, of course, the more directly passionate and less rigid Italian repertoire. Two of the artists who dominated the Met during the 1920's were constantly trying to do each other in: Beniamino Gigli and Maria Jeritza. Though they could acknowledge that their talents were not directly competitive, the tension was always there when they sang together. A typical sequence began during a performance of Giordano's *Fedora* on January 14, 1925. At the end of the second act, Jeritza threw herself at Gigli like an offensive guard leading a play for the Chicago Bears. The unprepared tenor was impelled forward until he had to brace himself against one of the wings to keep from diving into the orchestra pit. In the next performance she wiggled like a newly-caught fish in his arms during the big love scene, causing him to lose his balance and stagger around while the audience giggled; and another time, as Gigli was paying her a formal call in Act II and accidentally dropped his top hat, she kicked it across the stage. It was all a lot of laughs, but so far they were all hers. On the night of January 26, Gigli had his turn, although he always maintained it was accidental. In the last act he pushed his tormentor so that she skidded into the footlights, spraining a wrist. Jeritza, of course, made a big thing about it in the press, calling him "murderer" and similar polite epithets despite an official statement from Gatti-Casazza declaring the whole thing unintentional. Both artists categorically refused to sing together again, but, as a matter of fact, they *did*, in *Tosca*. It was a fairly well-behaved if strained outing until the Act III curtain calls, which developed into a hassle just this side of a riot. In desperation Giuseppe Bamboschek, who was minding the store, routed Gatti out of bed to solve the situation. These nocturnal emergencies being hard on the health, Gatti finally agreed that the two artists needn't sing together any more, thus relegating another feud backstage.

Tosca, incidentally, has seen a lot of in-fighting between the soprano heroine and the baritone singing the villainous Scarpia; one struggle reached a rather messy climax when Tosca stabbed Scarpia with a banana instead of the prescribed paring knife. It made his death look a little hokey, to say the least, but his cries of rage were probably real enough. There's no record of why this particular baritone was singled out for a sloppy waistcoat, but the chances are he had spoiled the soprano's big aria, "Vissi d'arte." The two of them are alone on stage at that point, and the baritone is supposed to look vaguely interested and not interfere until the applause dies down. All too often, though, the temptation to draw at least a little attention to himself gets the better of the typical Scarpia. Thus, when Eleanor Steber was on her round-the-world tour a few years ago she sang Tosca in Zagreb with an otherwise all-Yugoslavian cast, the baritone member of which was an up-stager from way back. As soon as "Vissi d'arte" began Steber noticed a strange noise that soon proved to emanate from Scarpia's shoes. He was pacing back and forth at a furious clip squeaking loudly at each step. She tried to keep her mind on her music, but the squeaks were difficult to ignore, especially when the villain walked completely off stage momentarily so that the noises continued from behind a piece of scenery. Miss Steber, being a self-contained artist, got through the performance in fine style without committing mayhem, but it is Scarpias like this who *ask* to be stabbed with a banana.

About a dozen years after the Gigli-Jeritza set-to, Metropolitan subscribers were treated to another donnybrook, this

time between Grace Moore and Polish tenor Jan Kiepura.
Throughout his brief local operatic tenure the two of them
carried on a singularly bitter feud that often erupted on
stage. When she would go for a high note, he would pinch
her; when he extended his arms at the end of an aria she
jabbed him in the ribs. The essence of the argument is perhaps
exemplified by the struggle over the chair in *La Bohème:*
all through rehearsals they fought over the position of this
piece of furniture, Kiepura trying to force Moore ever further
upstage, and it continued right into the performance. They
shoved the chair back and forth, upstage and down, until
finally the soprano, gathering her strength, jammed it down-
stage and sat in it, all in one motion, thereby winning the day.

When Clara Louise Kellogg's career was in full bloom,
prima donnas almost invariably owned their own costumes,
as some do to this very day. She was particularly fond of the
costumes she wore as Violetta in *La Traviata;* it was therefore
a considerable blow when she discovered that the tenor she
was singing with one season had chronically dirty hands and
was forever ruining her pretty clothes. She bore the finger-
marks as long as she could, but then her natural fastidiousness
as well as her womanly pride prompted her to write him a
note requesting that he wash his hands before performances.
He replied via an intermediary that he'd be glad to, if she
would supply the soap. She did for an entire season.

If dirty hands can be an annoyance, how much more up-
setting can be the singer who sprays his music. When the
contralto Emily Lablache substituted once as Donna Anna in
Mozart's *Don Giovanni* she wore her own costumes, only to
find herself opposite the tenor Brignoli, one of the more
notorious expectorators of the time. During the trio of the
maskers the first few rows of the house heard the soggy
Lablache whisper loudly to him in French, "See here, my
good friend, can't you for once spit on Donna Elvira's dress?"

The upstager, of course, is still with us. He—and it's most
often a he—quite deliberately tries to focus attention away
from wherever it happens to be back to where he feels it
rightfully belongs: on himself. Leonard Warren, a very great

artist indeed, was also a past master at this sort of thing, able to steal a bow by adroitly sweeping up a thrown bouquet of flowers, sniffing them, then gallantly handing them to the prima donna for whom they were intended in the first place. In the second act of *La Traviata* he once completely stole a scene away from the suffering soprano by deftly inveigling her into a game of Alphonse and Gaston on the small stairs that formed the center of the set. He was good at it, and also subtle. Some of his colleagues have been as subtle as meat-cleavers. One of them, a tenor renowned for his high C, for some time had the habit of muttering comments to his co-stars calculated to keep them off balance. "Watch out," he'd say, "here comes the B flat. Well, you got it again. You'll never get it next time . . . ," and so on. It could get pretty disconcerting. On tour with the Met one season he was chattering away in this fashion at a mezzo-soprano during the second act of Verdi's *Il Trovatore*. Staying in her character as the Gypsy-woman Azucena, she leaned towards him and said quietly, "Boy, in this opera I play your Mama. If you don't keep quiet I can easily slap your face right here on stage." He kept quiet.

This particular mezzo is as fond of *Carmen* as of any opera in her repertoire, which is true of any soprano who can manage the notes. There's always been a special magic about Bizet's masterpiece, and part of the magic has made this tempestuous heroine a breeding ground for many of music's more spectacular tussles. For some reason sopranos who sing the part wind up feeling possessive about it, even after retirement. Geraldine Farrar, who left the Met in 1922, apparently resented the publicity build-up that preceded Risë Stevens' first Metropolitan appearance in the role, commenting that "in my day artists became Carmen by *singing Carmen.*"

Farrar, come to think of it, was herself involved in a series of altercations while singing in *Carmen* with Enrico Caruso. In one performance, on February 17, 1916, she slapped his face in Act I and pushed a chorus girl roughly in Act II, all of which led inevitably to the climactic third act. Here she struggled with such enthusiasm during Caruso's music that he grabbed her wrist and held it. Farrar, naturally, bit him, whereupon he spun her to the floor in an exceedingly undignified posture. They were all smiles during the succeeding curtain-calls, but backstage the row continued unabated. She swore never to sing Carmen with her antagonist again, while Caruso insisted that she could sing all the Carmens she wanted, because he was through with Don Jose. It was all more or less a tempest in a teapot, though, because at the very next performance of *Carmen* the leading roles were taken by Farrar and Caruso, without the attendant acrobatics.

The soprano who almost single-handedly popularized *Carmen*, Minnie Hauk, was probably the originator of this tradition of high-handed gypsies. She was a difficult one regardless of the opera, and in *Carmen* this was especially true. In Boston on February 8, 1886, with Mapleson's company, her tenor was Luigi Ravelli. In the middle of Act III he was about to belt out a high note that invariably brought down the house when Hauk inexplicably rushed forward and threw her arms wildly around him. The note was choked off a-borning. Ravelli, understandably annoyed, tried to throw her into the orchestra pit. She got hold of his red waistcoat and held on for dear life while he shouted "Laissez-moi! Laissez-moi" until all his buttons popped off. Her hold now precarious, Hauk scooted off to comparative safety on the other side of the stage. "Regardez!" Ravelli declaimed in a stricken voice to the whole world. "Elle a déchiré mon gilet!"

The audience, convinced that it was all part of the show, applauded the unexpected realism of the acting. When the curtains closed a violent argument blossomed backstage, complete with threats and counterthreats. The following morning Colonel Mapleson received this letter:

Palmer House, Chicago
February 9, 1886

Dear Colonel Mapleson:

The vile language, the insults and threats against the life of my wife in presence of the entire company, quite incapacitate her from singing further, she being in constant fear of being stabbed or maltreated by that artist, the unpleasant incident having quite upset her nervous system. She is completely prostrate, and will be unable to appear again in public before her health is entirely restored, which under present aspects will take several weeks. I have requested two prominent physicians of the city to examine her and send you their certificates. Please, therefore, to withdraw her name from the announcements made for the future.

As a matter of duty, I trust you will feel the necessity to give ample satisfaction to Miss Hauk for the shameful and outrageous insults to which she was exposed last night, and Mr. Ravelli can congratulate himself on my absence from the stage, when further scenes would have occurred . . .

I am, dear Colonel Mapleson,

Very truly yours,
E. de Hesse Wartegg

The next day a lawyer's letter arrived, demanding bond against Ravelli on Hauk's behalf, which Mapleson had no choice but to grant. The next time the prima donna sang Carmen, her Don Jose was Signor De Falco.

Actually, Ravelli and Hauk did sing together again, more than once, but the results were always a little ludicrous. He was in constant terror of being throttled as he ascended to a high B flat, and she lived in mortal dread of the long knife that Ravelli carried and with which he had often threatened her. What resulted was a series of *Carmens* with long-distance love scenes, in which the heroine in the last scene would do her best to drop dead before the hero could approach anywhere near her with the pig-sticker demanded by the libretto. It was entrancing, but not exactly Bizet.

The most inventive Carmen, as well as one of the greatest, was probably Emma Calvé. She was a law unto herself who, as Marguerite, thought nothing of ruining the effect of Valentin's death (in *Faust*) by getting up and wandering across the stage. If she gave herself this kind of license in Gounod, the freedoms she took with *Carmen* can be imagined. She would constantly think up new pieces of business with which to bait her Don Jose at each performance. It was she, for example, who first popped a flower into her tenor's mouth just as he was about to begin his big aria, the Flower Song. One of her favorite gambits was to constantly drop little things all evening long so that Don Jose was forever stooping down to retrieve something for her. Of the few tenors who resisted her, the most successful was the memorable Jean de Reszke. During one performance Calvé almost littered the stage with odds and ends in a futile attempt to get Reszke to pick them up. He ignored the rubble completely, commenting afterwards, "Well, if she thought I was going to bend down and split my elegant brand-new tights she had better think again."

The perfect *Carmen* story involving these two artists may or may not be true. It is said that once Calvé got up and walked off the stage after de Reszke had stabbed her in Act IV. The furious tenor dashed in pursuit and dragged her back onstage from her dressing room by main force, only to have her get the last laugh by singing his last measures in unison with him. They bred giants in those days.

The ways of the musical world being what they are, many a supposedly vanquished worm has triumphantly turned. In the continuous internecine warfare victory is sweet but revenge is sweeter. Consider, for example, the glee that suffused the conductor Hans von Bülow after a trip to Bayreuth. He went to visit Cosima Wagner, the composer's widow and his own ex-wife, and was entertained munificently. On his departure a large throng came to see him off at the railroad station, all fussing over him, the daughters of the family kissing him, everybody making a great to-do. As the train chugged slowly away, Bülow leaned far out of his compartment window, waved, and shouted, "But there is still one greater: Brahms! Brahms! Goodbye, goodbye!"

Sometimes revenge has been completely impersonal. Fyodor Chaliapin was roundly detested by the crew backstage at the Metropolitan because of his high-and-mighty ways, but they had few opportunities to do anything about it. One of those opportunities came during Massenet's *Don Quichotte,* an opera the Russian basso particularly enjoyed. The stagehands who hoisted him up onto his mule also contrived to stick the animal with something sharp, so that Chaliapin's entrance was made on a bucking, snorting, kicking beast. He had all he could do to hold on, let alone make like a star. The evening, as far as the crew was concerned, was a huge success.

Sometimes simple excellence can turn the tables. When Tetrazzini was in Petrograd the machinations of one of her rivals forced her at the last minute to sing Gilda in *Rigoletto*, which she hadn't done in years, instead of Rosina in *The Barber of Seville*, which she had rehearsed. There was nothing to do except fake her way through the performance as best she could. Her big aria, "Caro nome," terrified her, but she was helped through it by the promptings of the tenor Masini, singing the Duke, who hid on stage. When the aria was completed Masini forgot himself completely, jumped up and shouted "Brava!" From his position on stage he led the ovation. Tetrazzini's evening was a triumph, which completely ruined the power play of her unnamed adversary—who, as a matter of fact, left Petrograd immediately afterwards.

The most professional revenge of all was exacted by the tenor John Braham, a colleague and rival of Elizabeth Billington at the start of the Nineteenth Century. They were singing together in Milan in Nasolini's florid *Il Trionfo de Claria* when it all happened. The applause Braham got during rehearsals infuriated Billington's new husband, M. Felican, who conspired and plotted until he persuaded the conductor to leave out the big tenor aria on the night of the first performance. Braham was taken totally unawares by the change, but somehow word of the scheme had leaked out to the audience in advance, as such things often do, and the omission was loudly booed. Next day Signor Gherardi, the manager of the company, announced in the bills that Braham's scene would be performed on the second night, and so it was, to a fine ovation.

Braham, however, was not about to let the matter rest here. Still angry, he planned his retribution carefully. All arias in those days were expected to be embellished with improvised ornamentation by the singer. It was well known, though, that

Billington's embellishments were never spontaneous, but were carefully worked out beforehand and then committed to memory note for note. Once set they were never changed. Braham therefore, memorized all her roulades at the first performances and, as soon as he could, he used all her fioriture in *his* big aria, which came before hers. The prima donna, listening in the wings, was dismayed but helpless. Unable to improvise, and not daring to repeat the ornamentation her rival had just used, she sang her aria absolutely straight, without a single grace, much to the audience's surprise and displeasure and her own shame. At the next performance Braham let her off the hook, but she refused to sing the duet with him. It was some time before they made up.

This affair alone would be sufficient to guarantee Braham's entry into whatever corner of Paradise is reserved for singers. If not, let it be noted that he and Elizabeth Billington later became close friends, which *must* prove something.

Chapter 4

The Prima Donna Versus the Audience

THEATRE HAS been defined as an audience, some actors, and a platform. Add music and you've got opera. The delicate relationship between the first two of these factors is what spawns the phenomenon of the prima donna.

Audiences are easily as temperamental as any star, and the interplay between them has been on occasion spectacular. Many of the biggest names have tried to avoid any unnecessary contact whatsoever with the public, probably on the theory that distance lends enchantment. Thus Olive Fremstad, when she sang Venus in Wagner's *Tannhäuser*, would make her final appearance of the evening (in Act III) wearing street clothes draped in a mass of pink chiffon. She would exit, shed the drapery, toss off her wig, clap on her hat and be half-way home before her fans could start crowding backstage.

Naturally, there were times when even the resourceful Madame Fremstad found herself in close quarters with enthusiasts. After a Sieglinde in *Die Walküre* she was cornered by one who gushed, "I used to be so confused by Wagner, but tonight I really believe that I understand it all!"

Fremstad impaled her admirer with a cold smile. "Isn't that nice?" she replied. "You are more fortunate than I who have given my whole life to the study and still know so little."

The Divine Olive was dealing from strength. She had both tremendous popularity and the honest talent to deserve it; with few exceptions audiences were on her side. An aroused public *can* be terrible in its wrath, aroused opera-lovers in particular. In the Italian city of Parma they once even went so far as to get the local police to escort an unloved Carmen to the railroad station to make certain she left town as soon as possible.

Italian audiences are notoriously the most volatile, perhaps because the art is such an integral part of Italian life. Nowhere else is it likely that a leading tenor will be sufficiently infuriated to leap off the stage into a box to wreak his vengeance on a heckling spectator, as happened not long ago in Naples. The opera that night had been *Il Trovatore,* the tenor was the brilliant and strikingly handsome Franco Corelli, and the situation was far from unique in Italian opera annals. In defending his honor in this direct fashion, Signor Corelli was acting in an ancient tradition; some of his predecessors have actually become involved in duels, of which one, involving the wild castrato Caffarelli, was simply to uphold the supremacy of Italian opera over French. For the record, Caffarelli emerged unscratched after severely wounding his Parisian opponent, which presumably settles *that* dispute for all time.

The sex of the performer makes absolutely no difference when the ire of the aficionado is roused. As many sopranos have felt the bite of a barrage of hisses as have tenors, and recourse to physical revenge is denied them. Madame Albani, a famed 19th-century star, was a tranquil person who had a more-or-less tranquil and successful career. Nevertheless, she experienced the full fury of the Milanese when she became hoarse during a performance of Donizetti's *Lucia di Lammermoor* at La Scala. Not partial to foreign artists treading their boards under the best of circumstances, the public had a field day. Hisses and shrill whistles descended upon her head from all over the auditorium, the noise getting louder as the evening dragged on. Finally the tenor, being nobody's fool, walked off, leaving her to face the barrage of disfavor as best she could alone. She kept going until just before the Mad Scene, the climax of the drama, and then, gathering all her dignity together, she calmly turned her back and strolled off the stage. The curtain fell a few moments later on a scene of utter chaos. Albani firmly declined not only to go back on stage that night, but to fulfill any further part of her La Scala contract.

This Pyrrhic sort of victory, while satisfying, does tend to cut down on the number of places a singer can perform, as some of our present-day divas have discovered. It should be invoked only when lesser measures fail, and even then only when it's certain who is being booed. Marcella Sembrich, the Polish coloratura who was a leading star at the Metropolitan until 1909, was singing the Queen of the Night in Mozart's *The Magic Flute* in Chicago when she heard loud hisses upon her entrance for her second big number, the "Vengeance" aria. Assuming that the audience had turned upon her, she fled from the scene and refused to sing. What had actually happened was that Giuseppe Campanari and Fritzi Scheff, the Papageno and Papagena, had received a tremendous ovation for their scene, and the applause was continuing into Sembrich's entrance music. Some members of the audience had begun shushing the applauders, and Sembrich took the "shshshsh" she heard to be directed at her.

Seldom are the artists mistaken, though. They are extremely sensitive to nuances of audience reaction. Perhaps even more devastating than being hissed is being laughed at, as was the soprano who created Violetta in the world premiere of Verdi's *La Traviata,* Fanny Salvini-Donatelli. She was a good singer, but with a figure somewhat less than svelte, and the thought of this all-too-ample matron dying of consumption convulsed the first-night audience. The effect on Madame Salvini-Donatelli has not been recorded, but the effect on *La Traviata* was unquestionably disastrous.

Just in passing, it might be mentioned that some demonstrations of disapproval have not been altogether spontaneous. The institution of the claque, or paid applause-leaders, firmly entrenched for centuries, has two edges. A man can as easily be hired to hiss as to cheer: many often have been. The first performance of Vincenzo Bellini's masterpiece *Norma* (at La Scala) was ruined by a disturbance caused by temporary employees of the wealthy Marchesa Bianchi, whose infatuation the composer had failed to requite. This cheerful little practice seems now to be falling into some disrepute, although there was an alleged outbreak even at the Metropolitan during a fairly recent soprano-tenor rivalry; when it does appear it's usually easily spotted for what it is.

Getting back to the Case of Madame Albani's Revenge, let it be noted that her tearing up a Scala contract is comparatively small potatoes compared to the larger-than-life vendettas some singers have sworn against certain opera houses, cities, even whole districts.

Amelita Galli-Curci, one of the most successful prima donnas of the Twentieth Century, was asked to sing in a revival of Bellini's *La Sonnambula* at La Scala. Milan was her native city, and she accepted with pleasure. It was only then that she was informed that Rosina Storchio (the first Madame Butterfly) had already been engaged for *Sonnambula* and would sing the leading soprano role of Amina. Mingardi, the Director of La Scala, offered Galli-Curci the second soprano part, Lisa. She stood as tall as her little frame would allow, looked at him silently for a moment, and then said, "Dear Mingardi, don't forget this: I shall never put my feet again in this theatre." She never did.

Even the sweet-tempered and charitable Swedish Nightingale, Jenny Lind, could hold a grudge. After her first triumphs in Stockholm, she went to Paris to study with the awesome Manuel García, full of ambition and bursting with confidence. García was not particularly excited by her voice, but he admired her diligence; for a year they worked hard together. It was at this time Giacomo Meyerbeer heard her sing. The composer of *Robert le Diable* and *Les Huguenots*, then the most popular musician in Europe, thought that Lind was fabulous. He immediately arranged for her to audition at the Paris Grand Opera. To Lind's immense chagrin, she apparently failed the audition: at least no job was forthcoming. Meyerbeer, almost as surprised as she was, used his influence to get her a debut with the Berlin Opera as Norma, whereupon her career took off like a rocket. However, she never forgot or forgave her mortification at the hands of the high moguls of the Paris Opera. Years later, when she was an acknowledged prima donna assoluta throughout the world, she took immense delight in refusing to sing in Paris, music capital or no.

By all odds the most celebrated feud between a star and an audience was that between Caruso and his home town, Naples. The young tenor had been scoring consistent successes for a couple of years at such widely scattered locations as Milan and Russia, and he looked forward eagerly to the day he might triumph at his own beloved San Carlo Opera. He had of course sung in Naples earlier in his career, at some of the smaller theatres, and had done pretty well (although on one occasion he had to face the unnerving sight of all his rival tenors staring at him from the first row, which they had bought out). Always, though, he had San Carlo as his goal, like all true Neapolitans. The opportunity came in 1901.

Unfortunately, Caruso neglected—or refused—to pay the accepted pre-debut calls on the leaders of two rival factions of noble playboys. This breach of usual procedure didn't help his cause any: these well-heeled opera bums (called, collectively, "The Syncophants") were a vindictive lot. On the night of his debut in Donizetti's *L'Elisir d'Amore* San Carlo was jammed to hear the heralded new tenor, and in the crowd were dozens of Syncophants, clustered around their respective leaders. At the first appropriate place, one of the factions applauded Caruso mildly, whereupon the other faction took this as *their* cue to hiss. The inevitable tumult followed hard apace, culminating in loud nasty language and a near brawl. Things quieted down soon enough, and the performance continued, but Caruso's debut at San Carlo was ruined. He took a frigid bow, deeply hurt by his reception, and received less than overwhelming acclaim. So wounded was he that he swore furiously: "I will never again come to Naples to sing; it will be only to eat a plate of spaghetti." It was a vow he kept, although he did return home to die and pedestrians walking past his house may have heard his final vocalization.

Naples was not the only city to bear the weight of Caruso's displeasure. In 1903 he sang for the first time in Barcelona. The opera was Verdi's *Rigoletto*, and things began well: after the Duke's first aria, "Questa o quella," Caruso was cheered vociferously. Shortly after, though, the audience began hissing him. The tenor was stunned, offended. He continued singing as well as he could, and after the aria "La donna è mobile" he was again applauded and cheered. If *that* was the kind of game these Spaniards played, he figured, he could play as well as they. He stubbornly refused to sing an encore.

What was left of the evening was pretty much of a disaster. The audience was mad at Caruso, and he resented them. After the final curtain he sulked backstage as the paying customers stalked out of the theatre in silence. All in all, an uncomfortable debut.

Into the tenor's blue funk barged the impresario, loudly demanding that Caruso sing all future roles in Barcelona at half the agreed-upon price. This was not exactly the most propitious moment to choose for this kind of haggling, although something must be said for the manager's promptness. Caruso, feeling far from charitable, rose up to a storm of indignation. Not only would he not lower his fee by a blessed cent, but he would sing only one further performance, the second *Rigoletto* which had already been announced. After that, nothing—at *any* price. That second evening was almost identical to the first, with the tenor being subjected to alternate cheers and boos, applause and catcalls. The infuriated Caruso vowed never to sing in Barcelona again. Needless to say he kept his oath, and then some: years later he turned down engagements at Madrid, 350 miles away, because of its proximity.

Parenthetically, New York has cause to be grateful that Caruso didn't take the lukewarm reception accorded his 1903 Met debut so much to heart. It was in *Rigoletto* again, with Antonio Scotti and Marcella Sembrich, and the tenor got only polite attention from the audience, with the critics carping at his "tiresome Italian mannerisms." His later triumphs justified his patience.

As indicated earlier, not every argument between a singer and the public resolves itself into lifelong ostracism, despite what both sides must at times consider ample provocation. For one thing, not many singers can afford to close doors behind them. For another, these affairs are usually only skirmishes, not wars, and when the dust settles the prima donna is often more firmly entrenched in popular favor than ever.

In 1813, the usually staid English public went on a rampage, and the cause was a prima donna, the adored Angelica Catalani. She had charm, a beautiful voice, fabulous technical facility, execrable taste, and no moderation. When she indulged in the accepted practice of ornamentation of her music, which was all the time, the original melody would vanish amid a welter of trills, roulades, and assorted folderol. Worse, the embellishments were usually unlovely at best, serving only to show off her agility. Allied to her unmusicianly attitude was an incurable egomania: when she ran the Theatre des Italiens in Paris for a brief spell she drove it to the verge of bankruptcy by her policy of huge salaries for herself and nothing for sets, costumes, or the rest of the cast. She figured it was Catalani the public wanted to hear, which most of the time was absolutely true.

Her drawing power in England was immense from the time of her glittering debut there in 1806 until she left the country in 1813, despite frequent sieges of bullheadedness. Apparently the British public would put up with the wildest sort of caprice in return for the privilege of shoveling out vast sums of pound sterling to hear Catalani warble. By 1813, though, even this long-suffering group had been strained to the edge of patience.

While appearing in London that year, Catalani failed to show up on two successive nights for which she had been announced. On the first evening, the audience accepted the inevitable: this wasn't the only time she had used this weapon in salary disputes and despite some grumbling the substitute performance went on instead. On the second night, though, audience discontent boiled. Catalani's absence was not to be borne twice in a row. The English may be slow to anger but they are decisive once aroused, and this night they became aroused. The smothered fury broke loose when the opera that had been substituted for the Catalani vehicle was about half over, at which point loud noises, generally impolite, began to rise from the audience. Soon the musicians, bravely fiddling away through it all, were drowned in a sea of cacophony. From the din emerged occasional clarion demands for the hide of Catalani, the manager, and assorted other miscreants.

The management, becoming a little alarmed, trotted out a small unit of armed military police that had thoughtfully been provided "in case," and which now rather nervously began to guard the apron of the stage. This precaution struck many of the gentlemen in the infuriated audience as a direct call to action, and dozens of them vaulted up to the platform. The self-conscious soldiers were easily overwhelmed. With the stage now in their victorious grasp, the spectators unleashed their vengeance on whatever was handy. Fixtures, mirrors, furniture and costumes were smashed and piled up into a huge heap in the middle of the stage. Settings were ripped. Real weapons and props alike joined the growing mountain of trash. By now, of course, the musicians had long since given up and scooted out of the way of possible destruction without bothering to gather up their instruments: a forlorn oboe and a consort of viols hence crowned the rubble. With nothing left to pile up, the mob decided it had accomplished its purpose, and everyone went home feeling better, except the manager. The theatre had to be closed for a week, with total damages amounting to over a thousand pounds, a pretty whopping sum in 1813.

The story has a postscript. When Catalani did condescend to sing again, she was greeted with a standing ovation.

The wrath of an audience, especially if organized, is a difficult thing to stem. The great prima donnas have managed to accomplish it, though, in varying ways and usually to their benefit. Marietta Alboni was without question one of the finest artists of the middle Nineteenth Century and one of the great contraltos in history. Rossini himself took her under his wing during the days before her formal debut in Bologna in 1842. Her career was almost without exception triumphant. However, in Trieste once she got wind of a plot to hiss her off the stage at her next appearance. Her well-informed source also supplied her with the names of the chief conspirators and the location of the tavern where they usually met.

Alboni was nothing if not direct. Putting on men's clothing, she set out to confront her enemies on their home ground. The transvestite deception was easy enough for her to carry out: she was of robust stature to begin with, had a naturally deep voice and none-too-feminine features, and wore her hair short. At any rate, the masquerade worked. She went to the cafe she'd been told of, and there sure enough were all the conspirators holding a full-cry conference at one of the tables. Alboni sat down at an adjoining table to listen for a while, then leaned over and joined the conversation.

She intimated that she (he) could not help overhearing that there was a trick about to be played on someone, and as she (he) was as fond of practical jokes as anybody, how about taking on a new partner? The men accepted her immediately and joyfully as a brother intriguer. She was informed that the cheery little group planned to hiss an opera singer off the stage that very night; wouldn't that be fun? Alboni allowed as how it might be worth a chuckle or two, but wanted to know what this particular singer had done to be singled out, so to speak. It turned out that the object of their attentions had actually done nothing, except that as an Italian she'd been singing in Vienna and Munich to Germans; this evening's festivities were planned as an object lesson in the consequences of unpatriotic conduct of this sort. Everybody agreed that the punishment fit the crime. The disguised contralto was given a little whistle and told that at a given signal at the end of Rosina's big aria (the scheduled opera was *The Barber of Seville*) the noise would begin. She (he) was to

join in with the whistle. Everybody shook hands, and th
intrepid Madame Alboni, clutching her whistle, departed.

That night the theatre was packed with an enthusiast
throng. The opening numbers were greeted warmly. The
Madame Alboni, looking quite feminine in Rosina's curls an
petticoats, made her entrance. Almost as soon as she ha
started her recitative a few of the plotters began making
disturbance without waiting for the signal. Calmly the prim
donna walked to the footlights holding up the whistle, whic
was now hung around her neck on a ribbon. "Gentlemen
she said, "are you not a little before your time? I thoug
we were not to commence whistling until after I had su
the aria."

There was silence for a moment, and then the house w
swept with a huge ovation led, be it noted, by the erstwhi
conspirators.

Of course, Alboni was a star, a species that almost l
definition can take care of itself. The second-rater often fac
a far tougher time at the hands of the audience with few
inner resources upon which to draw in moments of cris
There are exceptions, though. During the 1880's there was
tenor named Armandi who was, on his best days, awful. I
made his living by dashing all over Italy fulfilling contrac
other tenors had pooped out on. It was one night in Parm
one in Bologna, another in Milan, always as a substitute f
somebody else. Finally even Armandi wearied of the grin
After much argument he finally talked a manager in Napl
into giving him a six-night contract, which to this travel-sc
singer, used to invariably getting canned after a single p
formance, seemed like a lifetime.

He prepared diligently for his first appearance, which w
to be as Pollione in *Norma,* but it didn't do much good. I
was terrible. The Neapolitan opera-lovers, not the most patie
in the world, took it as long as they could and then began
make their dissatisfaction audible. In a few minutes the hissi
completely drowned out poor Armandi. When Act I fina
ended, he came out in front of the curtain, got the audienc
attention and begged them to leave him in peace for the r

of the opera, at which time he would leave the city. Otherwise, if they kept hissing, he swore that he would sing the remaining five nights of his contract.

The candor of the unfortunate tenor won even these hard hearts. Armandi not only finished the opera but remained for all six of his scheduled performances, getting roundly applauded each time. It was the high point of his career.

In Parma, that most demanding city of all, they still tell the story, perhaps even a true one, of the not-so-good tenor who came to sing Cavaradossi in *Tosca*. He made a hash of his first aria, "Recondita armonia," and received a bare smattering of applause mixed in with which was an inexplicable call from the topmost gallery for an encore. The tenor smiled a successful smile and, stepping to the footlights, obliged with a second rendition of the aria that was if anything less rewarding than the first. This time the applause was virtually nonexistent, except for the same gentleman in the top gallery who clapped again and called out loudly, "Encore! Encore!" Once more the overjoyed singer repeated his horrible performance. The hush that followed this third butchery was ominous, until once again the same voice called down, "Encore! Encore! You'll sing it until you learn it!"

The real front rank stars have never hesitated to take on the audience en masse—like Emma Calvé who held up 3,000 people for twenty-five minutes before a Met *Cavalleria* until the boxes were sufficiently filled to satisfy her. Caruso was singing in *Rigoletto* at Covent Garden one night when the Prince of Wales was in one box and ex-King Manuel of Portugal in another. The tenor was, unfortunately, in bad voice (*Rigoletto* again) at this performance, and at the opening of Act III, Manuel leaned over the rail of his stage box and said in a loud, clear voice, "Signor Caruso, are you going to start to do some real singing now?"

The conductor, who was the late Sir Thomas Beecham, stopped the orchestra. Caruso signaled him to go on. Strolling over to the ex-monarch's box, the tenor leaned negligently on the railing and, without once looking at Manuel, sang like an angel. He then deliberately turned his back on His ex-Majesty, snubbing him in truly regal fashion, as he continued to sing magnificently without a glance at the royal box.

Luisa Tetrazzini, one of the greatest coloraturas ever to turn a phrase, was similarly direct, if a little more imaginative, in a similar situation. She was scheduled to sing *Lucia di Lammermoor* in Puebla, Mexico, when just before curtain time the stage was flooded by the classic combination of rainstorm and leaky roof. Tetrazzini went on, but tried to keep her gown from being ruined by holding it up a few inches out of the sloshing lake on stage. The performance was not many minutes old when she heard a lady in a box say out loud, "Just fancy! A prima donna attempting to emulate a high-kicking ballet-girl!"

Tetrazzini waded as near to the woman as possible and sang, to Donizetti's music: "Madam, you are shocked, very shocked, I know it, yes I do. But do you know the stage is soaking wet and our dresses all are spoiling, yet just to please you I am ready, perfectly ready, to let my dress drag through the wet and be completely ruined if you, dear Madam, will promise to buy me a lovely new one." It even ended on a high note. Those in the audience who realized what was going on laughed, but the original offender sat with her back to the stage for the rest of the act, then left. The remainder of the performance, complete with skirts held above the water, went on without comments from in front or interpolated poetry from the stage.

The place of the press in the lives of singers is an ambivalent one. While many of them pretend to ignore what the professional critics have to say, that's largely sham. In truth, for good or ill, newspapers are the single most important part of the public, able to help or hinder a career enormously, and everybody in opera is keenly aware of the fact. Many a performance is aimed not at the audience as a whole but at the dour gentleman in the sixth row center who will dash out before the beginning of Act III in order to make his deadline. The power of the press cannot be gainsaid.

In the usual course of events, there's not much recourse an artist has if the reviews are bad. It's not cricket to belt the critic in the teeth or complain to the publisher, no matter how great the temptation. Besides, it's generally more politic to try to make friends with him so that the next time around he might be inclined to be a little less severe in his judgment. Most critics, despite rumors to the contrary, are human.

Perhaps the simplest and most direct critique of all time was offered to Dame Nellie Melba subsequent to her first public recital. She was six years old and the concert took place at the Richmond Public Hall in Australia. Little Nellie started with "Comin' Through the Rye," following it with a song her grandmother had taught her called "Shells of the Ocean" which for effect she performed from a precarious perch atop a high stool. The next day she eagerly sought the opinion of one of her impressed playmates, who said in a shocked voice:

"Nellie Mitchell, I saw your drawers!"

Not all reviews are so brief, pithy or ingenuous. As a matter of fact some have even angered the singer involved sufficiently to call for direct action, regardless of the consequences—as when the tenor Giacomo Lauri-Volpi punched an offending critic squarely in the nose—although the action is usually non-violent. Usually, but not always.

Lilli Lehmann tried to quit the Berlin Opera in 1880 because of a dispute with the management over getting the title role in Meyerbeer's *Dinorah*. While everybody waited for a decision from the Kaiser (who alone had the authority to grant her request to leave the company), a local tabloid printed a little item purporting to reveal the "truth" behind Lehmann's request for discharge, the "truth" being that she was in what used to be called an interesting condition. The public was not only interested in the condition, it was fascinated, and l'affaire Lehmann became the talk of the town. It would have been embarrassing enough to the diva had it been a factual report, but it wasn't, which made her slow burn at not being able to get in to see the editor of the scandal sheet all the warmer. She camped on his office step, finally, until with the support of a gentleman friend she ultimately confronted the yellow journalist in his lair. By this time Lehmann's anger was uncontained, and she boxed his ears with all the strength in her not inconsiderable frame. The net results were a retraction, a black-and-blue editor, and a substantial boost in Madame Lilli's popularity.

Mostly, though, prima donnas get their innings in less physical fashion—when, that is, they get their innings at all. Olin Downes, for years the dean of New York's music critics from his eyrie high up in *The New York Times,* once objected in print to the German of mezzo-soprano Risë Stevens as evidenced in her performance as Octavian in Strauss' *Der Rosenkavalier.* Soon after the review appeared, Miss Stevens was seated next to Mr. Downes at a formal dinner party. She blithely chattered away at him in German until he said, "I'm sorry, but I don't speak German."

"Well," said the singer triumphantly, *"I do."*

A formal dinner also provides the setting for one of the choicest comebacks ever attributed to an opera star. Mary Garden was seated opposite the noted industrialist, politician and after-dinner speaker, Chauncey Depew. Throughout the evening he kept staring down her low-necked dress until finally she asked what it was that he found so hypnotizing. He replied, "I am wondering, Miss Garden, what keeps that gown up."

"Two things, Mr. Depew," she said; "your age and my discretion."

Chapter 5

Baton, Baton, Who's Got the Baton?

ONE OF THE FEW absolute rulers left on the face of the earth is the tyrant of the pit and the podium. Things have come a long way since Handel directed his own orchestra from the harpsichord, until we are now faced with the phenomenon of the virtuoso conductor. He is typically a man of excellent skills, forceful personality, and extraordinary temperament who in his wilder moments can pale the deepest purple outburst of the most flamboyant prima donna. Because of the very nature of the calling, conductors tend to feel a little removed from the rest of mankind, a little closer to the angels. After a particularly rousing concert at the helm of the Boston Symphony Orchestra, Serge Koussevitzky, one of the finest, was accosted by a tearful fan who blubbered, "Maestro, you conducted just like God!"

Koussevitzky, weeping himself, answered, "Yes! And think of the responsibility!"

The exalted position enjoyed by today's conductor has less than a century of tradition behind it; supreme though he may be his authority is not yet unchallenged. Board members, unruly orchestra players, noisy audiences, difficult impresarios and—most of all—singers may sometimes appear to the harassed baton-wielder to be in league against him. The continuing necessity to re-assert control has led to some of the choicer incidents in musical history. In earlier days when lines of battle were first being formed, contests of this sort were pretty elemental, without much subtlety. Thus, when Sir Michael Costa was summoned to the hotel room of the tenor Masini in order to go over *Faust* because Masini didn't feel like appearing at rehearsal he simply refused, sending the tenor into a high dudgeon and thence home to Italy. Should a present-day singer show similar audacity most conductors would probably indulge in either a full-blown rage or a full-grown witticism, neither of them calculated for far-reaching effect. An exchange far more likely now than the wordless Costa-Masini encounter took place in San Francisco not too many years ago. Leonard Warren was rehearsing for *Falstaff*, and at one troublesome point he stopped the proceedings, walked to the footlights, and said, "Maestro, do you mind if I show you how I sing this?"

The conductor's riposte: "Mr. Warren, do you mind if I show you how Verdi wrote it?"

Certainly the most celebrated operatic conductor of our century has been Arturo Toscanini, who not only established his personal authority firmly and early, but maintained it despite the onslaught of generations of prima donnas. From the beginning he set the very highest of standards for himself, insisting that his colleagues try to live up to them as well. He became as a matter of course the most demanding of disciplinarians, with the most volatile of temperaments. He would never condone the prima donna instinct in anyone but himself.

Once when he was presiding over a rehearsal at the Metropolitan he corrected a phrase just sung by Geraldine Farrar, who without comment proceeded to repeat it precisely the same way. Toscanini stopped the music again, a dangerous glint in his eye, but before he could say anything Farrar declared, "You forget, Maestro, that *I* am the star."

He peered at her for a moment, then spoke very quietly: "I thank God I know no stars except those in heaven which are perfect."

The music, of course, was sung his way. Had his reply not

had the desired effect, he was quite capable of resorting to open rage if needed, or to nastier remarks. Enshrined forever in the memories of those who heard it was his furious attack on a buxom soprano who had been making a number of musical mistakes: "If you had up here what you have down there, what a singer you would be!"

Obviously, Toscanini's career was studded with battles. Singers being what they are, and the Maestro what he was, battles were inevitable. The results were invariably worth it, but as a by-product he left among his legacies an almost inexhaustible mine of material for biographers.

One of his early skirmishes was also one of the most memorable, if for no other reason than that Toscanini's opponent was another titan, Enrico Caruso. Furthermore, the occasion was the tenor's La Scala debut in the season 1900–01. His first performance was to be as Rodolfo in *La Bohème* opposite Emma Carelli with Toscanini in the pit. Rehearsals were going fine until in going over his first-act narrative, "Che gelida manina," Caruso sang the high C falsetto. There seemed to be no real reason for it; although he had relied on falsetto earlier in his career he was by this time accustomed to using his full voice at rehearsals, as was expected in Italy. Perhaps he was nervous, perhaps it just slipped out. Whatever the cause, when Toscanini stopped the rehearsal to ask him for more voice on the high note, the tenor got stubborn about it. They went over the aria again, again the C was delivered falsetto, and when Toscanini inquired as to the whereabouts of the strong high note he had asked for, Caruso answered airily, "I don't feel like singing it just now."

This not being a reply exactly calculated to calm the Maestro's nerves, the rehearsal continued with an enraged silence from the podium. Nobody mentioned the matter for the next two rehearsals either, although Toscanini was obviously controlling his wrath with difficulty as Caruso continued to "save" his voice. Finally, after the third rehearsal the conductor told the tenor he could lower the note a half-tone if he wanted to, but he *must* sing at full volume. Period. No arguments permitted. Caruso nodded. The next time, though, he sang at half-voice as usual.

Toscanini halted the music. After contemplating the miscreant balefully for a moment, he coldly informed the cast that there would be a special rehearsal at five o'clock the next afternoon. There he had the cast read through *La Bohème* in reverse order, starting with Act IV, then Act III, Act II and Act I, and this time Caruso sang everything in the fullest of voices, including the offending high C. The conductor was obviously pleased, but nonetheless called *another* rehearsal for 9 P.M. that night. Caruso, who figured he had already given in, was livid: he was prevented from exploding only by the calming words of Emma Carelli, who assured him that the entire cast would sing half-voice at the next run-through.

However, when the curtain rose at 9 o'clock it revealed to the weary cast an auditorium almost filled with an invited audience of local civic and musical dignitaries, as well as all the first-string music critics. Carelli and the rest of the cast were so thrown by this unexpected throng that they completely forgot any promises they may have made and sang out as if it were opening night. Caruso though, tired, feeling betrayed, stubbornly sang half-voice. The distinguished audience stirred as in the pit Toscanini's blood pressure rose dangerously. The first-act love duet was a farce, what with Carelli blasting unremitting fortes for all she was worth and Caruso crooning away, until the curtain mercifully fell.

During the intermission Gatti-Casazza rushed backstage to beg the tenor for more voice, but Caruso stoutly maintained that he had just eaten dinner and couldn't possibly sing any louder. Sure enough, in Act II he continued along his solitary falsetto way. Toscanini listened for a few pages, then stopped the orchestra, declaring: "If you don't sing in full voice, I can't go on."

Caruso made excuses, argued, worked himself and Toscanini into such towering rages that the conductor threw down his baton and marched out of the pit as Caruso stalked angrily off the stage. Throughout La Scala consternation bordered close to horror as the infant season teetered on the edge of ruin. Deputations of leading citizens were sent to each of the dressing rooms to no avail until Gatti broke the ice by calling on the services of Duke Visconti di Modrone, leader of Milan's aristocracy and president of the Scala Board of Directors. The Duke brought all his considerable charm to bear on the grumbling tenor until at long last he got him to reluctantly emerge from his dressing room and resume the rehearsal. Simultaneously similar pressure had been exerted upon Toscanini, who scowlingly mounted the podium again. The run-through, hardly a roaring success, dragged to a conclusion at one A.M.

The next morning, not surprisingly, Caruso awakened feverish and sick. Unfortunately for the management of La Scala, so did the tenor Borgatti, who was to sing in *Tristan und Isolde* that night. *Tristan* had to be canceled and *La Bohème* was substituted, but there was Caruso, *that* opera's leading tenor, also incapacitated. Gatti was nothing if not hard-headed; firmly believing that Caruso's fever was more temperamental than bacterial, he led a delegation to his sickroom. They pleaded and begged: La Scala had to open that night as it always had, the opera had to be *Bohème*, so therefore he had to sing. Caruso wasn't quite so sure that he followed this line of reasoning, but the persistent Gatti-Casazza finally persuaded him to appear. La Scala's tradition was upheld, but the tenor's debut was something less than sensational.

Relations between Toscanini and Caruso, though respectful, never became exactly warm.

That Caruso stood up to Toscanini, right or wrong, sets this incident apart. Few conductors have been so Olympian in their wrath. He could wither the most hardened performers, most of whom preferred to remain unwithered. When Frances Alda went to La Scala to debut in *Louise*, being given its local premiere in Italian, she sang through the entire score before Toscanini asked her politely what language she had been singing in. She stormed off for several days, but the whole thing ended amicably when he agreed to coach her in the words.

Once, he conducted a rehearsal of Meyerbeer's *Les Huguenots* which went dreadfully. Everything was bad, especially the tenor, De Marchi, who hid unhappily in the wings as Toscanini climbed onto the stage mad at the world. The conductor scolded everyone he could find, particularly bawling out the lighting men. De Marchi, reaching for an out, seized this opportunity. "Bravo, Maestro," he exclaimed. "This darkness is a real outrage. It caused me to sing a bad note. Those electricians are beasts. The blame is all theirs!"

The greatest of singers confessed to undergoing a special strain when performing under the Toscanini baton. Lotte Lehmann sang with him for the first time in February of 1934, on an hour-long broadcast which featured her as soloist in "Abscheulicher!" from Beethoven's *Fidelio* and "Dich, teure Halle" from Wagner's *Tannhäuser,* a difficult pair of selections under any circumstances. It was a brilliant occasion, but one that drained Lehmann emotionally. Her next appearance was as a Lieder recitalist before the Beethoven Association, and as she was about to enter she whispered to Erno Balogh, her accompanist, "Oh, I feel so calm. An easy program, a nice appreciative audience, and no Toscanini there to be frightened of."

They came out onto the platform, bowed—and there in the front row, beaming benignly, was Arturo Toscanini. Lehmann later said that at that moment her voice and her breath deserted her simultaneously.

For all his difficulty, Toscanini was a man beloved by many, and admired deeply by more. He and the composer Giacomo Puccini were extremely fond of each other, although they carried on a feud nonetheless. "That man is a pig," said Puccini; when Toscanini conducted an opera by Catalani, he said, "That pig always loved Catalani more than me. But when I think how he conducted the premiere of *La Bohème* at Turin and *The Girl of the Golden West* in New York, then it seems I must forgive him all his sins. But he is a pig nevertheless."

Puccini forgot (naturally) to remove the "pig's" name from his Christmas list, so that Toscanini received the gift bread that the composer had had his baker send to all his friends. When he heard about it, Puccini sent him a telegram reading, "PANETTONE SENT BY MISTAKE. PUCCINI."

The next day an answer arrived: "PANETTONE EATEN BY MISTAKE. TOSCANINI."

The most delicate relationship that a conductor must establish is that with the players in his orchestra. It was in this area that the Maestro's extraordinary musicianship served him most nobly. His first rehearsal with the Metropolitan Opera orchestra before his 1908 debut was of *Götterdämmerung*. He introduced himself, then began conducting without the score as was his habit. After a few bars he stopped and told the first cellist, "That note should have been B flat." The cellist bristled. "No, that's not what I have here, nor have I ever had it. In all the years that I have been playing I have always played the note as A natural."

"Well," said the Maestro, "you have always committed an error. I see I have not convinced you. Would you like to have me get the full orchestra score for verification?"

The cellist insisted that, yes, he *would* like to see the full score. It was brought. The note was found. It was—what else?—B flat. Amidst the admiring hubbub, Toscanini resumed the rehearsal, once and for all in complete command of an orchestra that never again questioned his authority.

This sort of omniscience was commonplace in his career, but even hardened observers like Gatti-Casazza and Richard Strauss were amazed when he went through *Salome* for the first time, scoreless, and when asked if there had been any mistakes could honestly reply, "Of course not. If there had been errors I would have stopped."

Of course, the rapport between Toscanini and the musicians, while profound, was rarely all sunshine and roses. Quite to the contrary: his rehearsals were usually stormy affairs, punctuated with wild rages and bitter invective. During his tenure with the N.B.C. Symphony he once furiously ground an expensive watch to bits under his heel on the podium. The radio network solemnly presented him with a large batch of dollar watches, which he just as solemnly accepted. One by one they all crumpled under his wrathful heel.

However much he may have done for the watch industry, the Maestro's most normal recourse was to good old-fashioned tongue-lashings. In La Scala at the turn of the century a musician's union was being formed, during the nascent days of which he was conducting rehearsals of *Götterdämmerung*. At the first orchestral run-through, he halted in the middle of the Norn scene and said, "Well, have you organized your union?"

"Si, Maestro."

"And who is your president?"

"Peretti, the first trombone."

"Well, then, Peretti, you are certainly preparing your rules and by-laws?"

"Si, Maestro, they are in preparation."

"Good. I beg you, set down Article One, the members of the orchestra must always play in tune. Do you understand?"

"Si, Maestro."

"I say this because today, for example, you played out of tune in so indecent a manner that worse is impossible." And with that, the rehearsal proceeded successfully to its conclusion.

While going over some Beethoven one day, Toscanini rapped for silence just after one of his players had finished a solo passage, then musingly tapped the baton against the side of his nose before finally calling the player's name. The musician stood up. "Yes, Maestro?"

"Tell me please, when were you born?" The mystified man told him. "And in what month?" He was told the month. "And what day?" The player, now thoroughly upset, thought for a moment.

"I think," he managed to get out, "that it was Tuesday, Maestro."

Triumphantly, Toscanini shouted, "THAT was a black day for music!" Immediately he raised his baton. "And now, da capo!"

While most of the time tactics like this had the desired result, Toscanini occasionally went a little too far, a circumstance intensified in this country by his sometimes quaint grasp of English. At one session he so singed the ears of his first trumpet player that the musician, angrily leaving his place in the orchestra, shouted at him, "Nuts to you!"

Toscanini gazed at the back of the departing trumpet-player quizzically for a moment, then called after him, "It's too late to apologize!"

Incidentally, Toscanini was far from the most vitriolic conductor to emerge from the Italian opera houses. That honor was probably held by Leopoldo Mugnone, already noted for his acid tongue when Toscanini was still a cellist. Once he gave one of his violinists, who was having a singularly bad day, a dreadful going-over. The violinist demanded a little respect: he was, he stated, the brother of the great composer Leoncavallo. "But how can one respect you," sneered the conductor, "you who are neither 'leone' (lion) nor 'cavallo' (horse) but an ass!" It was also Mugnone who shouted up from the pit to the soldiers on stage who were about to "execute" a particularly bad Cavaradossi in the last act of *Tosca:* "Soldiers! Use real bullets!"

For all of Toscanini's tantrums, for all of his driving, his sense of purpose was so great and his results so superior that orchestras generally preferred to work with him than with any lesser light. One orchestra even resorted to conspiracy and fraud to get him back. It happened at La Scala when Gatti-Casazza was the manager.

Although Toscanini got on more or less famously with audiences, it was quite a while before he made the Italians abide by his dictum of "no encores under any circumstances." In 1903 he was conducting Verdi's *Un Ballo in Maschera* with Giovanni Zenatello when the audience refused to let the opera continue after the tenor's big aria in the second scene. Toscanini waited patiently for a while, but they kept shouting for an encore. Finally he threw his baton at the howling mob and left the theatre, not to return for three years; his anger carried him all the way to Buenos Aires.

Casting about for an adequate replacement, Gatti came up with Cleofonte Campanini. He was earnest enough, but not in the same league. Things didn't go too well for him, and people blamed him for a variety of ills including the horribly unsuccessful world premiere of *Madame Butterfly*. The members of the orchestra became most disenchanted of all. Delighted as they may have been for a short while to be out from under Toscanini's hard yoke, they now longed to have him back. Accordingly, they hatched a plot that was simplicity itself. The next time they performed the Overture to *Tannhäuser* they all played one-half tone lower than the written notes, a transposition that Campanini completely failed to notice. It's difficult to say at this late date whether this was a major reason, but the fact remains that he was fired not long thereafter. Gatti perforce ended his quarrel with Toscanini as soon as the Maestro returned home. It was years before they had another serious fight.

Musicians were not the only targets of Toscanini's shotgun fury. He could get mad at almost anybody if the situation warranted anger, as it often did. Perfection is an elusive goal; its pursuit can be harrowing. Although the Maestro had no illusions about his abilities in non-musical fields, he nevertheless had sufficient taste to know the good from the shoddy in matters of stage decor and deportment, so that some of his more tearing passions were flung at designers and directors.

During those treasured days when he was conducting at the Salzburg festival one of the revivals was to be *Falstaff*. On the day Toscanini saw the sets for the first time he sat quietly until he saw Ford's house, then bolted out of his chair and exploded towards the door. The designer and the top brass of the festival charged off in hot pursuit while Toscanini screamed at them: "Shame! Do you call *that* an Elizabethan house? You know nothing, nothing! Go read what Verdi says in the score. No! This is not a theatre; it is a place for the ingnorante! I will not conduct in such a place. No! No! Never! Never! . . ." His voice getting more piercing as rage threatened to choke him, he dashed out the exit, throwing his overcoat over his head to avoid being photographed.

The directors of the festival held a hurried meeting as Toscanini took a soothing drive in the country. When he returned a message awaited him to the effect that an authentic Elizabethan house would be constructed for Master Ford. Next day, the placated conductor saw the new set and said only, "Ecco!"

Somehow Toscanini, like Professor Higgins in *My Fair Lady*, always thought of himself as a thoroughly reasonable man, never realizing that anyone as passionately devoted as he was to certain high ideals could hardly escape intense emotional involvement. When he was about 75 a quarrel arose between two members of his fine N.B.C. Symphony which he promptly offered to mediate. Probably because they didn't dare refuse, the two disputants appeared in his dressing room to argue their cases. Toscanini heard one through, then turned politely to the second. Midway through his story the Maestro got red in the face, shouting "STOP! You are not saying the truth! You are not a *man*! You speak lies!" Before the astonished musician could say anything, Toscanini began punching him in the head. Finally he broke for the door, running wildly to the elevator and safety with the conductor running right after him intent upon further assault. It took a brace of N.B.C. employees to lead the still fuming Maestro back to his dressing room. It was hardly a text-book case of mediation, but at least no one could accuse him of equivocation.

Like all great men Toscanini earnestly believed in the rightness of *his* way, but it was always the music that counted, not the proving of a point. He could and did yield when the end result would be thereby improved. A cherished memory for Helen Traubel, and a warm note upon which to leave the Maestro, was provided by a disagreement they once had. He suggested a certain emphasis be changed, then stopped and thought about Traubel's interpretation again. He smiled his delightful smile and said, "Cara, you are right and the old man, he is wrong."

Miss Traubel, conveniently enough, provides a bridge away from the perennially fascinating career of Toscanini. When she arrived in New York prepared to conquer the world she found all the doors closed to her. She was absolutely unable to get a major audition anywhere in the city. Finally she was introduced to John Barbirolli, who was to conduct the Philharmonic, by Maestro Giorgio Polacco; of necessity it was done informally at Traubel's residence. She sang for him and he immediately offered to do Brünnhilde's Immolation Scene from Götterdämmerung with her in the fall, a break which she eagerly accepted. Later, however, when the young conductor had gone, she said to Polacco, "He wants me to sing the Immolation Scene!"

Polacco was unperturbed. "So?"

"So I don't know it."

"So neither does he," Polacco shrugged. "Don't you tell him and he won't tell you. You both have plenty of time to learn it."

In 1961 another of the giants passed. Sir Thomas Beecham hid his vast talents behind a raffish attitude, an air of irascibility, and an extraordinary wit. His death deprived us at once of a superlative conductor and an entrancing human being.

Among the many remarkable things about Sir Thomas was his incredible poise. He could carry off the most difficult situation without once being ruffled. He made his American debut as a guest conductor of the New York Philharmonic in 1928, and after his opening concert the audience was surprised to see him walk off the stage with a weird mincing gait. He later explained to his friends that his suspenders had given way in the middle of the performance, forcing him to hold up his trousers with his left hand while conducting with his right. Nothing daunted, he finished in fine style, albeit a little lopsidedly.

Not content with an unconventional exit, a few years later he made an unconventional entrance, this time to conduct the Philadelphia Orchestra. Suffering from gout, he was pushed to the podium in a wheelchair.

It was Sir Thomas, too, who once got so carried away with the music he was directing that he fell off the podium. In a typical remark, he subsequently claimed that "podiums are designed as part of a conspiracy to get rid of conductors": he thenceforward insisted on having a railing behind him.

Not even an apparent musical faux pas could faze him. In the salad days of his own opera company he once decided to conduct a particular performance himself. He arrived in the pit, acknowledged the applause, then opened the large score he had brought with him. He leaned towards the concert-master and whispered, "We are performing *Figaro* tonight, are we not?"

The concert-master blanched. "Oh no, Sir Thomas, it is *Seraglio*."

"My dear fellow," Beecham said, "you amaze me!" He then closed the score he had brought and proceeded to conduct the complete performance from memory.

In dealing with orchestras, Beecham was unlike anyone else. He would rarely rant or exhort, but would rely on his own special blend of mischief and pomposity. Thus, the simplest directive could be blown up by Beechamesque hyperbole into this classic: "At Figure 19, cymbals, a grand smash of your delightful instruments to help in the general welter of sound, if you please." And offending instrumentalists would not be blasted with invective, but might be coldly invited "to have the kindness to keep in touch with us occasionally." It got results, too.

The one struggle in which his sang-froid sometimes deserted him was that against rude and inattentive audiences. These he could not bear, and often throughout his career he would shush them from the pit, or even shout imprecations at them. The time he conducted *Fidelio* was not unusual: he was using the Mahler version, in which the Prison Scene blends directly into the Third Leonora Overture. As might have been expected, some of the Covent Garden crowd applauded at the wrong place. Sir Thomas spun around furiously and shouted, "SHUT UP, you fools!"

There came a time when the audiences he so roundly belabored decided to exact revenge. One evening when he came out he received no applause. After the first piece nobody clapped. The surprised Beecham went on to the next selection, and again there was no applause. He proceeded to the next piece and, when once again he was greeted with stony silence he turned to the crowd, bowed his head and said, "Let us pray."

It is perhaps superfluous to add that the audience once more became his.

Beecham was a first-rate opera conductor and loved it, but the field nevertheless called forth his most scathing commentary. Once, before he was to lead *Götterdämmerung*, Lady Cunard suggested to him that for this performance he might best use a score, so as to remember all the rhythmic changes. He fixed her with a twinkling glance and answered, "There are no rhythmical changes in *Götterdämmerung*, my dear Emerald. It goes on and on from half-past-five till midnight like a damned old cart horse."

Poor singers, with whom he was often inflicted, stimulated some brilliant sallies, as when Sir Thomas insisted that he had made the Covent Garden orchestra play loud enough to drown out a particular cast "in the public interest." It was also at Covent Garden that he was conducting when, in the Triumphal Scene of Verdi's *Aida*, one of the horses in the procession committed a grievous social error. Beecham turned to the audience and said, "A distressing spectacle, ladies and gentlemen, but gad, what a critic!"

Aida again, this time at the Metropolitan: he had an ensemble played over again at rehearsal while he sat back and listened. When it was finished, he shook his head in amazement. "Gad!" he said. "Just like the Salvation Army!"

As indicated earlier, the greatest burden of temperament borne by conductors almost certainly is supplied by singers.

Not even being related seems to help. Luisa Tetrazzini was hired by her brother-in-law Cleofonte Campanini to sing *Lucia di Lammermoor* in Parma, an opera house noted for its fine harpist. As soon as Tetrazzini heard that this harpist had been known to get encores for her playing of the introduction to Lucia's first aria, "Regnava nel silenzio," she insisted that Campanini get rid of her. "What am I supposed to do until the harpist has finished her encores? Count the seats in the stalls?" She had her way.

Fyodor Chaliapin, a difficult man generally, was especially a trial to conductors. In Italy he once categorically refused to sing with a certain conductor who had the temerity to watch the score rather than Chaliapin, thereby missing what the basso considered to be a vital bit of business. He insisted that the public came to see him, not some conductor's back, which may have been true but had very little bearing on the case.

Many singers have resented injunctions against encores, but most of them have abided by the rules. Not so Chaliapin: on at least two occasions he helped himself to forbidden encores of his aria "Dormirò sol" in Verdi's *Don Carlo* by simply stepping to the footlights and telling the embarrassed conductor where to begin.

Come to think of it, the Russian basso was a piker compared to some of his colleagues and predecessors: the tenor Russitano once directed the orchestra himself for his third encore of "Di quella pira" in what must have been a pretty hairy performance of *Il Trovatore*.

In the wilder days before the Divine Right of Conductors was as well established as it is now, prima donnas once in a while would speak to the orchestra or correct the leader from the stage. When Lilli Lehmann was rehearsing an opera called *Carlo Broschi* in Danzig in 1868, she felt that an important scene in Act II was being paced much too slowly. Instead of waiting to discuss the matter, she called out to the conductor, Gustav Schmidt, "Quicker!" The startled Schmidt dropped his baton, and only the manager of the company could persuade him to continue with the rehearsal.

A case could perhaps be made for Lehmann having inherited her propensity for shouting instructions from her mother, Marie Loew, who was a singer and harpist. She once sang Desdemona in Rossini's *Otello* with Richard Wagner in the pit, accompanying herself on the harp in the last act Willow Song as was her wont. Somehow the orchestra got confused, which was nothing compared to the mess that Wagner seemed to have gotten himself in. He was totally lost. Loew saw him desperately flipping pages in the score backwards while the orchestra struggled on way ahead, so she called out loudly, "Further, further!" The audience thinking she had just screamed "Fire, fire!" began to panic. By the time the noise and tumult had died down, and everything was settled again, Wagner had found his place. The rest of the opera continued without incident.

Differences of opinion regarding tempo form perhaps the single most trying area of conductor-performer relations. A Metropolitan Opera ballet girl dancing in *Carmen* in Boston with Beecham directing got so upset at his rapid tempi that she removed a slipper and hurled it at Sir Thomas' head before fleeing offstage. Emma Calvé also used her foot to resolve a dispute. In *Cavalleria Rusticana* she loudly stamped out the time she wanted when the conductor refused to take her tempo. It was that same conductor, incidentally, who precipitated her departure from the Met. He was accompanying her on the piano at a Sunday evening concert when she asked him to transpose the music one tone lower. He refused, and she walked off the Metropolitan stage—forever.

There have been isolated cases where a feud between a singer and a conductor has at least indirectly led to the singer's success. Artur Bodanzky, one-time head of the Met's Wagnerian wing, once called the great Australian soprano Marjorie Lawrence "a kid who couldn't sing *The Ring.*" So determined was she to prove him wrong that she decided to go all out when she first sang Brünnhilde in *Götterdämmerung,* including actually riding her horse Grane into Siegfried's funeral pyre when she immolates herself at the end. She got her brother to be a "super" and hold the horse, and everything went beautifully. It was a triumphant climax to a triumphant evening.

The most satisfying story about conductors and singers concerns Richard Strauss. He was conducting *Tannhäuser* with Pauline de Ahna as Elisabeth when, during rehearsals, an argument broke out between them because he felt she was hurrying the tempo. The words got angrier and tempers hotter until she was shrieking insults at him from the stage, and the whole wild ruckus culminated in her heaving the piano score at him and running to her dressing room. The enraged Strauss stormed after her and bashed into her room without knocking, slamming the door behind him. A crowd gathered outside the door to listen to the furious noises and shrill insults coming from inside—then suddenly there was silence. The hush seemed dangerous. One of them, everybody figured, was probably dead. The question was, which one?

Into the curious throng came a delegation of orchestra players. The leader knocked on the door, which was opened by Strauss. The prepared speech came stammering out. The orchestra was so horrified at the terrible behavior of Fräulein Pauline de Ahna that they felt they owed it to their honored conductor Herr Richard Strauss to refuse ever again to play in an opera in which she had a part . . .

Strauss remained silent through the whole presentation, smiling. When it was over, he said, "That hurts me very much, for I have just become engaged to Fräulein de Ahna."

The course of true love, they say, never did run smooth.

Chapter 6

Eat, Drink and Be Merry, for Tomorrow You Sing

THEATRICAL PEOPLE in general are a little larger than life, and opera stars especially so. They do things in a grand manner, accentuated by the giddiness of the ascent to the top and the equally giddy possibility of descent to the bottom again. Idiosyncrasy is raised to a fine art. Gestures are magnificent, and sometimes a little wacky.

After the scrimping days of his beginning, Enrico Caruso enjoyed lavishly the rewards of his career. He would order perfume by the gallon, Tiffany gew-gaws by the dozen, expensive Russian lace in twenty-yard lots—and these are neither exaggerations nor isolated occurrences. His press agent once told him that his jewels were as fine as Diamond Jim Brady's. "Better!" Caruso snorted, sulking for the rest of the day.

One of the prizes of success in the world of music is the ability to travel in style. The tenor Masini went to South America with an entourage including a personal secretary, undersecretary, cook, valet, barber, doctor, lawyer, journalist, agent, and treasurer. They provided a nice homey touch besides being a handy traveling claque. The great baritone Mattia Battistini never transported less than thirty large trunks, which contained among other things a complete costume change, down to the socks, for every act of every opera in which he appeared. These two, Masini and Battistini, probably hold the international championships for unwieldy travel arrangements, but there are several close contenders even among today's stars, airline weight-limits to the contrary notwithstanding.

Some artists, though, have gone precisely in the opposite direction, towards parsimony. The more success, the less money they are willing to spend. Just recently a celebrated coloratura soprano was to have been greeted at the Dallas airport by a large contingent of dignitaries but got to her hotel ungreeted because she had come tourist class, which exits from the airplane via a different door. The most renowned miser in operatic history, however, was almost certainly Francesco Tamagno.

On his first trip to America, Tamagno traveled on the same ship with his employer, Maurice Grau, who had as usual provided his artist with first-class passage. As the trip proceeded Grau began noticing that he wasn't seeing much of Tamagno. In fact, he hadn't seen him at all. Finally getting worried, he had a search instituted. The tenor was uncovered in the second-class section, where he had been holed up ever since he had turned in his first-class ticket for a second-class one, pocketing the difference in price. To Grau's horrified protest, Tamagno righteously replied, "I am a democrat and it gives me pleasure to travel second-class, where one has more freedom and does not have to observe all the formalities of first-class." The manager fought, but it was useless. Tamagno always thereafter held him up for the money for a first-class ticket though actually traveling in more modest fashion.

His colleagues were invariably astonished by Tamagno's pinch-penny habits. Although they should have been used to it by then, Jean de Reszke and Nellie Melba were still a little shocked when, at a luncheon tendered by the Millionaires Club, he calmly stuffed his napkin with candied fruit, almonds, chocolates and a bunch of orchids from the centerpiece, wrapped it all up and carted it home.

Some time after this, the conductor Luigi Mancinelli gave a luncheon for Melba, Tamagno and a few others at an Italian restaurant. The main dish was veal cutlets á la Milanaise, which everybody attacked with gusto. There were, however, a few cutlets still left over at the end. Tamagno leaned towards Mancinelli, indicated the derelict veal, and said, "What are you going to do with them?"

The conductor was bewildered. "Do with them? Nothing!"

"Ah!" said Tamagno; then, to a waiter: "Give me a newspaper." When the paper arrived he carefully wrapped up the left-over meat, explaining to the fascinated table, "You see, my little dog—he loves veal cutlets."

The next day, Mancinelli happened to call on Tamagno in his rooms at lunchtime. The tenor and his daughter were just sitting down to a meal of veal cutlets a la Milanaise.

Food has been a matter of prime concern to many prima donnas, perhaps because of the hunger that threatened them when their careers were beginning. Some of them have been valiant trenchermen indeed, as witness the fabulous contralto Ernestine Schumann-Heink. She was eating a huge steak in a restaurant one day when Caruso came over and teased, "Are you going to eat that steak all alone, Tina?"

She looked at him gravely and answered, "No! Mit potatoes and vegetables and some spaghetti."

Various artists have had assorted ideas about the proper dietary preparation for operatic singing. Some refuse to eat anything until after a performance, but Lillian Nordica had a full dinner served to her in her dressing room *before* she went on, and Brignoli would consume large quantities of raw oysters while awaiting his cue. Frances Alda, at least during the early part of her career, stuck to a nutritional ritual. Every day for breakfast she would have porridge, kippers, tea, toast and marmalade. For a mid-morning snack, to assuage that empty feeling, she would consume a dozen raw oysters and a bottle of stout, and then for lunch on non-singing days she'd have a rich-sauced chicken stew. On days when she was going to sing, the luncheon menu was changed to a large tartar steak (raw chopped beef with chopped onions, a raw egg, capers, and olive oil). After all, a girl has to keep her strength up.

The culinary habits of singers sometimes had effects other than the intended ones. Clara Louise Kellogg claimed that she could often identify the tenor she was singing with by the odor on his breath alone. Stigelli, she said, reeked of lager beer, while Mazzoleni bore the aroma of the two pounds of cheese he usually ate on performance days. When it came to garlic, though, all she could tell was that the source was invariably a tenor. The drinking of beer particularly bothered Miss Kellogg when it slowed up matters, as it did when the lager-guzzling Belgian conductor Ryloff stopped a rehearsal, saying "Boys, I *must* have some beer," and went to a nearby saloon while everybody waited.

Actually, the drinking of beer is a time-honored operatic custom. Grisi, among others, loved it. Late in her career, when she tired easily, she relied upon beer for its restorative powers. In Donizetti's *Lucrezia Borgia*, in which she took a big fall, she arranged for a glass of foaming brew to be handed up to her through a trap door in the floor while she lay prone. She would chug-a-lug it down with her back to the audience.

All sorts of liquids are relied upon by all sorts of prima donnas for backstage vocal first-aid and accident prevention. Mary Garden drank a glass of milk with ten drops of iodine in it after each performance, which still ranks as the least palatable of all panaceas. Among today's stars, Joan Sutherland drinks a sweet black-currant syrup called Ribena, Birgit Nilsson is fond of orange juice spiked with straight glucose, while Eileen Farrell makes do with sips of—ugh!—warm cola. You pays your money and you names your poison.

These liquids, of course, do serve the very valid function of keeping a hard-working singer's throat moist, although sometimes people can get to rely on things like this too strongly. There was once a tenor who absolutely had to have a lozenge in his mouth while singing or, he was convinced, he wouldn't be able to utter a note. During one performance he dropped the lozenge and signaled frantically for his valet, who was standing in the wings, to give him another one immediately. Unfortunately, the valet was fresh out of lozenges. Thinking quickly, he ripped a button off his jacket and handed it onstage to the singer, who popped it into his mouth without looking at it. Sucking away at the button, he sang superbly. Later, when he discovered the nature of the evening's lozenge, the shock cured him of his dependence.

This tenor's concern with his throat was certainly not unique. Opera stars depend on the proper functioning of their respiratory tracts as baseball pitchers depend upon their arms: this is the way they make a living. It's not so surprising, then, to find many a singer going a little overboard when the well-being of a vocal cord is at stake. Jean de Reszke always carried a laryngoscope during performances, frequently using it. Perhaps the foremost health-fetishist of all was Olive Fremstad, who would have her dressing room visitors sprayed for "germs" before receiving them. A great believer in the efficacy of pine oil, she would fill her hotel bathtubs with hot water and pine oil and, much to the dismay of a number of railroad lines, would insist on draping her train compartments with wet sheets sprinkled with the stuff. It may not have done much good against microbes, but it definitely guaranteed her privacy. Whether or not the pine oil was responsible, Fremstad had remarkable breath control: whenever she went for a walk she would practice taking deep breaths, holding them as long as she could and measuring her success by the number of lampposts she could pass without having to gasp for air. With about two or three posts to a block, at a leisurely pace she could easily score up to five.

When Jan Kiepura walked anywhere he used to have his valet follow a few paces behind clutching an atomizer. Every once in a while the tenor would stop and open his mouth, whereupon the valet would dash up and give him a squirt. Without a word being said, Kiepura would resume his march while the valet fell into line, still a few paces back.

The reactions of most opera singers to extremes of weather are usually pretty typical of the rest of us, if more colorful.

The English tenor Sims Reeves would respond to hot London days by wearing a cork helmet to rehearsals—but the splendid Rosa Ponselle was different. Fair weather or foul, she liked fresh air and detested steam heat. As a matter of fact, she refused to allow any heat at all backstage at the Metropolitan on the nights on which she sang, having her secretary call up beforehand to remind the janitorial staff that Ponselle was on her way. When she arrived at the opera house she would feel the radiator pipes to make sure. One bitter cold night the engineer turned off the heat on the Fortieth Street side only, which is the side of the house on which the ladies dress, leaving the men's side, on Thirty-ninth Street, nice and warm. Unfortunately, Ponselle chose that night of all nights to come in via Thirty-ninth Street. One touch of the hot radiator convinced her that treachery was afoot, but, like all prima donnas, Ponselle was able to handle the situation with dispatch, if not calm. The steam was turned off.

Ponselle's desire for the open air even extended further: for a period she rode a bicycle from her home on Riverside Drive, down Broadway and Seventh Avenue, into the Thirty-ninth Street entrance and, on a memorable occasion, right into Gatti-Casazza's office. The novelty soon wore off, but it was invigorating while it lasted. The Met management, of course, had kittens thinking about the traffic and what it might do to one of the greatest stars ever to walk their boards, but that's the sort of hazard inherent in the trade.

To all singers, the voice is the unfailing barometer of health. If it's there, then all is well. If not, then watch out. When the tenor Brignoli fell off a moving train once (he was rather accident-prone) he was discovered by the rescue crew still flat on his back but singing lustily away. Convinced that his larynx was undamaged, he cheerfully reboarded the train while singing a prayer of thanksgiving.

Matters of medicine aside, singers boast the strangest sets of beliefs. Most of them would object if you mentioned the word "superstition," but try whistling backstage and see what happens. Brignoli, a fairly odd sort all around, refused to allow himself to be touched during on-stage love scenes, feeling it was both indecent and unlucky. Using similar reasoning, he traveled all over with a large stuffed deer head which he would hang in his dressing rooms. When he sang well he would hurry back and pat it, but on nights when he was off his form he would slap it around, cursing it in vivid Italian.

We may be somewhat removed from stuffed deer heads now, but a number of our contemporary greats still have toy animal mascots. Superstition or not, the fact remains that Elisabeth Soederstroem, the lovely and gifted Swedish soprano, carries with her everywhere a complete menagerie of miniature animals, many of them gifts from admirers, all neatly arranged in a small zoo-like box. They sit on her dressing table while she makes up. Renata Tebaldi is another diva who is toy-animal-collection-prone (hers are stuffed), and many others would not part under any circumstances with the one lucky item, like Lucine Amara's ancient teddy-bear. Even the men are not immune: far from it. Giorgio Tozzi, a great basso with fine intelligence, keeps as a mascot a small bronze snail named, for reasons he alone could explain, Emerson.

Miniature animals aren't the only objects that are supposed to bring good luck to prima donnas. Miss Soederstroem passionately believes in the usefulness of a little golden chain she wears on which is mounted a model of the Sacred Heart, and many an Italian star carries the three ancient Latin symbols of a tiny statue of a hunchback, a red horn of fortune, and a two-fingered ivory hand designed to ward off the evil eye. Olive Fremstad did everybody one better by traveling with a complete "homelike trunk" which was unpacked whenever she remained in one place for more than a day. It contained a whole grab-bag of familiar and treasured and lucky items, like shawls, runners, statuettes, pillows, and a framed photograph of Lilli Lehmann.

Sometimes superstitions require particular actions. Christine Nilsson would never go on stage unless somebody first "held her thumbs" for good luck; many performers, including the Met's Norman Scott, have knocked wood before entering; others have stepped on cracks in the floor. Metropolitan tenor

Barry Morell, following an old theatrical tradition, has his wife kick him before he makes his first entrance. While he feels it's been effective for him, he has complained mildly that "she obliges with great enthusiasm."

The personal spare-time predilections of opera stars provide a fascinating field for research, although not one entirely germane to this book. For no particular good reason, nevertheless, it's hard to resist telling of the time Maria Jeritza entertained Gatti-Casazza and other dressing-room visitors between acts of a *Die Walküre*—in which she was the Sieglinde—by turning somersaults in full costume and make-up. Or of the time the fine basso Andres de Segurola, who was teaching Frances Alda Italian vernacular but had not yet mastered the intricacies of English, proposed a toast thusly: "Alda, you permit? I speak on your behind . . ."

It's also hard, because of some of the difficulties encountered in interviewing opera people, to resist telling of the pervasive habit of tardiness. There are precious few prima donnas who are punctual, but it all fades into insignificance when compared with the notorious lateness of Mario, the Nineteenth Century idol, who was on time only once in his career. For that appointment he arrived a full half-hour early. It must be admitted that he was as puzzled by this strange lapse in his normal pattern as was anybody, but then he realized that he had misread his watch, thinking it was five minutes to twelve when it was actually only eleven o'clock. Had he read the timepiece correctly he would have been his usual thirty minutes late, a fact that reassured him no end.

It's not that Mario or any operatic personality rates the tag "indolent": far from it. As a group they are the most energetic people imaginable, working hard, traveling, studying —even socializing—with enormous vitality. It's possible that no other area of endeavor requires so much actual work, on both central and peripheral matters, as does opera. The phenomenal creative vigor of certain operatic composers is already legendary; it is said of Donizetti that while he was playing cards he got an inspiration, left the table and wrote

Edgardo's aria "Tu che a Dio" for *Lucia di Lammermoor*, then returned to finish the game. As a matter of fact, Donizetti wrote the entire last act of *La Favorita* in three or four hours. When he heard that Rossini had composed *The Barber of Seville* in thirteen days he remarked, "Yes, yes, he was always notoriously lazy!" Which, in some ways, was true, except that Rossini possessed such a remarkable fecundity of ideas that when he composed lying down, as he often did, if a completed page slipped off the bed he would compose an entirely new one rather than get up to fetch the fallen manuscript. That may be profligacy, but he had genius to waste.

One characteristic that runs like a leitmotiv through opera history is the fondness of prima donnas for pets, lots of pets, of all varieties from the tamest to the strangest. When Lauritz Melchior sent Helen Traubel a gift of two lion cubs from South Africa, he probably expected her to keep them, although the busy soprano sent them to the St. Louis Zoo where they were appropriately named Lauritz and Helen. Had she raised the beasts herself she would have been safely within a hallowed tradition that is still very vigorous indeed. To cite one example, the brilliant American mezzo-soprano Nell Rankin provided a loving home for a jaguar in her Manhattan apartment until it weighed well over three hundred pounds and tended to knock visitors down with the enthusiasm of its welcome. Miss Rankin's husband, prominent physician Hugh Davidson, has learned to take her enthusiasm for wildlife in stride. When he was first introduced to the then infant jaguar, soon to be named King Tut, he said philosophically, "I'm only glad it wasn't an elephant."

Minnie Hauk always had a special fondness for cats, although not necessarily for lions and jaguars and such. She had many ordinary-type cats during her career, naming them all Jenny Lind. She was in the habit of singing to them, usually "O luce di quest' anima" from Donizetti's *Linda di Chamounix*.

One of the more fanatic animal fanciers was the soprano Ilma di Murska, who was at the height of her career during the 1870's, but then, she was a little quaint about a lot of things. She spent most of her time training her very own traveling menagerie to sing. This might not have been so odd if she owned a flock of canaries, but she dragged along with her from town to town a miniature zoo that included parrots, magpies, cockatoos, monkeys, an angora cat and a large Newfoundland dog named Pluto. The dog was a particular favorite for whom a place was always set at di Murska's table. He would dine on capon and similar luxuries with, it is reported, excellent table manners. This in the days before Walt Disney.

The parrots were not quite as amiable as Pluto. Among other things, they seemed to have an aversion to silk or damask upholstery, especially in flowered patterns. They would carefully tear it to shreds if they weren't already using it as an unlikely site for a certain distinctly avian defilement. De Murska was always happy to pay for the damage caused by her pets; the way things were going she had plenty of joyful moments. Once though, in Glasgow, a parrot died (fed a piece of poisoned parsley by a parrot-hating colleague) and the prima donna called in two learned Scotch doctors for an autopsy. After a thorough examination they informed her that the bird had died of a surfeit of wallpaper, charging her three guineas for the opinion.

Adelina Patti was similarly parrot-conscious. Her bird, a remarkably clever one, could imitate her whistling of a number of tunes and speak several words and even complete sentences in English and French. One trick she taught him was found by Colonel Mapleson to be very disagreeable: whenever he came into the room the parrot would scream, "Cash! Cash!"

Lily Pons, the delightful French coloratura, is so fond of animals (she usually travels with a brace of dogs) that she turned a routine publicity gimmick into an all-day adventure. She was invited to have her picture taken while she rode the elephant at the Forest Park Zoo in St. Louis, which she did most happily, but instead of then going on about her business she remained at the zoo, making friends with the elephant and taking lunch—on a silver service, no less—with the chimpanzees in their cage. What's more, she skipped rehearsal the next day to return.

The devotion of prima donnas to their pets can go to great lengths indeed. Luisa Tetrazzini used to have a pet leopard which traveled with her. Once, in South America, he was riding in the luggage cart directly ahead of her when a jolt in the road shook loose his cage and he escaped down the street as fast as he could run, with Tetrazzini in pursuit. The wily leopard skidded sharply around a corner and into a small tailor shop. The startled proprietor, looking up from his sewing to be confronted by the baleful green eyes of a panting jungle cat, toyed momentarily with the idea of fainting but then rallied and scrambled up a ladder, screaming loudly as he climbed. The noise brought a policeman who became as dismayed as the tailor. A leopard on the loose in the middle of a peaceful city wasn't exactly covered in the police manual, but it seemed reasonably close to "inciting to riot" and therefore called for decisiveness. He drew his pistol and was about to shoot the animal when Tetrazzini dashed in, waving a fistful of money. The policeman accepted her offer gracefully, counting his cash while the prima donna began stalking her pet with bolts of the tailor's cloth until she had him entwined and returned to his cage. The tailor descended from his ladder to inspect the ruins of his shop, but Tetrazzini mollified him considerably by cheerfully forking over the large sums of money he asked in return for having entertained the leopard. As a matter of fact, he cordially invited her back, hoping that next time she might bring with her a whole zoo.

Chapter 7

Pride Goeth Before a Fall,
But Not Always

ARTISTS AS A GROUP are not especially noted for their retiring nature. Talent usually breeds an awareness of itself, and particularly in the performing arts people seem to have an acute realization of their own uniqueness. Of all performers, this is most true of opera stars. They have, to put the best light on it, never taken guff from anyone. Witness Chaliapin.

Fyodor Chaliapin is generally recognized as one of the greatest singing actors in history by all accounts, including his own. When asked what he would do if he ever lost his voice, he replied, "I would then be the greatest actor in the world." From his earliest successes on he maintained a remarkable self-confidence, no matter what the situation. It was in those early days, long before his international repute, that Chaliapin was commanded by Czar Nicholas II to sing for him at the palace of the Grand Duke Serge Mikhailovitch. The young bass did so, with what he considered excellent results. After the concert the Imperial family retired to another part of the palace to drink champagne. Shortly, the Grand Duke returned, carrying a gorgeous Venetian goblet on a silver salver. "Chaliapin," he said, "the Czar has asked me to offer you a glass of champagne to thank you for your singing, and so that you may drink His Majesty's health."

The singer drank, and said, "I beg that Your Highness will be good enough to tell His Majesty that Chaliapin is keeping the goblet in memory of this never-to-be-forgotten event."

There was nothing for Serge Mikhailovitch to do but keep wearing his frozen smile and exit carrying the tray and a large burden of noblesse oblige. As for Chaliapin, not only did he get away with the expensive glass, but later even had the nerve to ask for the remaining eleven in the set.

Royalty has never particularly fazed the prima donna temperament. An audience is an audience, and one impresario like another. In the 1730's the castrato Caffarelli was given a handsome jeweled snuff-box by King Louis XV of France. He sent it back because it wasn't adorned with the King's portrait. When told that only ambassadors received the royal portrait, he said, "Then let His Majesty make the ambassadors sing."

Caffarelli probably felt he was as much a king as Louis. In Naples, anyway, he ruled San Carlo despotically. He would hit other singers on the head if he didn't like the way they sounded, rewrite his music as he saw fit, shout to friends in the audience insulting comments about his colleagues who were simultaneously trying to sing. It was great fun, but finally even the patient Naples police had enough. In 1741 the "strutting capon" was tossed into the pokey for obscenity.

Caffarelli's relationship to Louis XV has had many an echo. Perhaps one of the most capricious artists of all time was the brilliant Eighteenth-Century soprano, Catarina Gabrielli. When she was asked by Empress Catherine II to sing at the Imperial Russian court, she demanded five thousand ducats. Her Majesty was shocked.

"Five thousand ducats? Why, I don't give more than that to one of my field marshals!"

The Empress of all the Russias should have known better. She got the obvious retort. Gabrielli got the five thousand ducats.

La Gabrielli's pride, allied to her wayward sense of responsibility, kept her on the brink of trouble throughout most of her career. When she was singing in Sicily the Viceroy himself gave a dinner in her honor. All the guests arrived except Catarina. After a decent interval, the Viceroy sent some servants to inquire after her. They found her at home, undressed and reading a book. She claimed that the Viceroy's invitation had completely slipped her mind.

Sicilian royalty was then marvelously patient, and this insult was overlooked, but after a while her insolence began to affect her singing. This no true Italian can forgive. After a series of sloppy performances, the Viceroy sent her a formal note demanding that she immediately stop singing sotto voce when performing at the Viceregal theatre. Gabrielli haughtily replied that she might be forced to cry, but not to sing. This struck His Majesty as being an excellent idea, and he had her arrested. As soon as she was locked up with the usual collection of felons, prostitutes, and bankrupts, she immediately proceeded to entertain them with her lavish talents, full-voice. She kept it up all day, every day, singing whatever the prisoners requested, with never a sotto voce note. Finally, twelve days later, she was released, followed by the cheers of her erstwhile fellow inmates whom she had entertained so— royally.

Gabrielli, incidentally, was not Catarina's real name. She was the daughter of one of Cardinal Gabrielli's cooks, and took the name of her patron. She was acting in a time-honored tradition. Many stars are known by purely fictitious names. Perhaps it helps create the façade that is so useful, although in some cases there is a legitimate reason. Young tenor Charles Anthony of the Metropolitan Opera has a real name that's *too* good: Caruso. Many names derive from cities of origin and provide a useful Italianate lilt. Thus Nellie Mitchell Armstrong became, courtesy of her great teacher Mathilde Marchesi, Nellie Melba, after the city of Melbourne, Australia, and Mary Louise LaJeunesse of Albany, New York, became Madame Albani. Sometimes there is a simple translation into Italian, as when Anne McKnight becomes Anna di Cavalieri. The classic operatic pseudonym of all time, though, belonged to a tenor named John Clarke who sang with Colonel Mapleson's company at the end of the Nineteenth

Century. He was a native of Brooklyn, and the name under which he ventured forth must have seemed exquisitely logical. He billed himself as Signor Giovanni Chiari di Broccolini.

John Clarke to the contrary notwithstanding, it's usually the female of the species that is the more vain, particularly about appearance. Conductors are an exception to the rule—Artur Nikisch used to wear white cuffs specially designed to show off his beautiful hands—but conductors are the exception to most rules. Sometimes early experiences in the careers of singers sensitize them. Emma Calvé, the great turn-of-the-century Carmen and Santuzza, never forgot a Cherubino she sang in a performance of Mozart's *The Marriage of Figaro* in Brussels shortly after her 1882 debut. Cherubino is a page-boy and wears, almost always, tights. Calvé was terribly ashamed of her thin legs and decided to hedge her bets by stuffing the stockings with cotton. It looked fine for a while, but as Act I proceeded Cherubino's constant activity caused the cotton to slip a little, then a little more. By the closing curtain the tights were a mass of strange-looking lumps, the audience was in hysterics, and the director was purple with rage. When Calvé made her entrance in Act II, it was without the cotton. The occasion marked the only time a pair of skinny legs got an ovation.

Many singers, of course, have been extremely attractive people. Seldom have they been unaware of the fact. In her autobiography, Mary Garden tells of her efforts to raise money for French opera and for Hammerstein, as part of which she had her portrait as Thaïs painted by Ben Ali Haggin and hung in Knoedler's window. She swears her portrait stopped the New York surface transit system as effectively as a good snowstorm.

The vanity of a great prima donna once saved her life. Giulia Grisi, one of the most successful sopranos of the Nineteenth Century, was married to the equally famous tenor Giuseppe Mario (born, by the way, Cavaliere di Candia). Their marriage was a good one, but not exactly tranquil. Among other things, Mario was wildly jealous; on one occasion he worked himself up into such a frenzy that he smashed everything breakable in the whole room, leaving a veritable carpet of shards and fragments. It was after one of these unnerving sessions that the despairing Grisi decided that the logical thing to do, all things considered, was drown herself. Being a creature of impulse, she dashed outside and headed for the nearest usable body of water. A friend breathlessly caught up with her just as she was about to do a one-and-a-half gainer into eternity. He tried all the standard arguments, pleaded with her, shouted at her, all to no avail. She was determined to jump, delaying only to savor briefly this last moment. The friend, an unidentified genius, then hit upon the only reliable course of action: he started describing to the pretty Grisi how horrible she'd look when she'd be fished out of the river, all bloated and muddy, with weeds in her hair. The weeds got to her. She didn't jump.

The sensitivity of prima donnas to comments about their beauty or lack of it has touched off many explosive incidents. Contralto Marianne Brandt, a pupil of Pauline Viardot-García, was sent to Bayreuth in 1882 to create the role of Kundry in the world premiere of Richard Wagner's music drama *Parsifal*. She was a marvelous artist, and an excellent reputation had preceded her. Nevertheless, at the first rehearsal, before she had sung a note, she overheard Wagner say, "she is impossible—the ugliest woman I have ever seen walk across the stage." Without further ado, Brandt packed her things and returned immediately to Munich, followed closely by Cosima Wagner, who begged her to return, and the rest is familiar: she triumphed in the role. One thing might be added: Wagner himself became one of Brandt's most ardent admirers, atoning for his earlier rudeness by making a public apology.

Like Brandt, most prima donnas seem to have amazingly acute hearing, especially when *they* are being discussed. Soprano Frances Alda, shortly after she had married Metropolitan General Manager Giulio Gatti-Casazza, was sitting in her box at the opera house and overheard voices in the next box. Otto Kahn, the Met's chief patron, was telling Henry Russell, director of the Boston Opera, that "as the Director's wife, it is much better that Alda should not sing here next season." The soprano stormed into Kahn's box and said, "I suppose it would be all right if I were his mistress instead of his wife. I resign right now." She actually didn't sing at the Met during the 1910–1911 season, concentrating on a concert tour and opera appearances in Chicago and Boston.

Alda may not have been the greatest artist ever engaged but she had a refreshing directness and a stubborn pride that made her attractive. As she put it, "the only difference between Frances Alda and every other prima donna is a few degrees of honesty." She was seldom loath to express that honesty. One summer she spent six weeks at Ganna Walska's château in France trying to teach that perennially hopeful incompetent to sing. She was paid ten thousand dollars for her services, but after a short while even this figure began to seem insignificant in the light of the immensity of the task. It was at a party that Alda's none-too-elastic temper finally snapped. Walska interrupted a conversation Alda was having with a visiting Princess by saying, "Ah, Princess, I see you know my singing teacher." The prima donna barked, "I may, for my sins, be trying to teach you to sing, but I am *not* your singing teacher. Remember that. I am Madame Alda."

The relations between established stars and comparative newcomers are usually, at best, delicate. In the 1890's, Lillian Nordica, already a well-known artist, met the fabulous Lilli Lehmann at Bayreuth and requested permission to call and pay her respects. Loudly Lehmann answered, "I am not taking pupils this season."

As a matter of fact, Lehmann *did* take some pupils, among them the great Swedish-American Isolde, Olive Fremstad. For all of Lehmann's virtues as an artist and a teacher, she cannot be said to have been a patient woman. During one of young Fremstad's lessons she flew into a towering Teutonic rage and hurled a heavy book of songs at Olive's skull. The terrified girl burst into tears and scrambled out of the room, heading for the front door. On her way she passed Lehmann's husband, the tenor Paul Kalisch. He was sitting at a table, holding his head in his hands, monumentally depressed.

"Olive," he asked, "what is the matter?"

"I will never come here again," Fremstad wailed through her tears, "she has thrown a book at my head!"

Kalisch sighed wearily. "Never mind, my dear. She does the same to me."

Fremstad survived the beaning and went on to greatness, but it takes a particular kind of fortitude to withstand the shocks that often accompany the teaching process. Sometimes a career narrowly averts disaster. Lotte Lehmann, one of the most beloved artists of the Twentieth Century, counts among the fortunate things that happened to her the fact that she was expelled from the Etelka Gerster School in Berlin. Her individual merits were completely overlooked there amidst the academic rigidity. Her particular teacher, Eva Reinhold, became convinced that Lehmann had no talent after she had once sung badly the Countess' aria, "Dove sono," from *The Marriage of Figaro*. With lunatic ferocity Reinhold had Lotte repeat "Dove sono" day in and day out for weeks on end until the young soprano grew to detest the sound of the introductory notes. To persist in the face of this sort of defeat is one of the marks of a star.

Not all the contacts between a rising generation and its elders are necessarily bitter. Quite to the contrary. Musical memoirs are filled with reverent and delightful confrontations as, so to speak, the torch is passed. Clara Louise Kellogg, the first truly American prima donna, who debuted in 1861, remembered with amused affection her first meeting with the great Madame Alboni, then very old and very, very fat. The young soprano told her, "Madame, I cannot tell you how honored I feel in singing on the same program with you."

Alboni replied, "Ah, Mademoiselle! I am only a shadow of what I have been."

An aura of self-confidence surrounds all the greats of the operatic world. Not only are they sure of their talent, they are usually quite certain of their ultimate success, no matter how difficult things may appear at the moment. Sometimes this very assurance makes the difference.

Even the fabled Dame Nellie Melba, whose life seems from a distance to have been one long golden chain of triumphs, had occasion to fall back on sheer nerve. After a season in Sicily in 1892 she returned to Paris en route, she supposed, to the Metropolitan. However, she was greeted there with the news that the interior of the opera house had been burned out and that there would be no 1892–93 Met season. Henry Abbey and Maurice Grau, the joint Managers of the company, told Melba that she had every legal right to claim her full contractual salary, season or no, but Dame Nellie proudly declined to try. It was a more courageous show of dignity than anybody knew: at that moment she had a grand total of two hundred pounds to her name, no job, and no immediate prospects. Deciding that a best defense is a good offense, she did what most great stars would do in similar circumstances. She went to Nice for a Riviera holiday. Not only that, she stopped in the finest suite at the finest hotel and took with her *two* maids instead of her usual one. All before Diners Club, too.

As luck (or design) would have it, Grau was also staying at Nice that month. He had of course no idea of Melba's financial straits, and when he decided to ask her to sing at the local opera he approached her with respect and the certainty that she would refuse. The diva, concealing her eagerness behind a massive show of indifference, allowed as how she might sing a performance or two, just to while away the time. Grau expressed the company's delight at being able to obtain her services, and promised to get her four thousand francs a performance.

Melba smiled. "Oh, I wouldn't dream of singing for less than five thousand," she told him.

She got it.

Dame Nellie at the time of l'affaire Nice was already a world celebrity, but it's possible to spot the easy confidence of many a star-to-be long before anyone has heard of them.

They are born with a certain sureness that success merely confirms.

When Caruso was a total unknown, he came to the composer Giacomo Puccini to get a recommendation to sing Rodolfo in his opera *La Bohème*. Puccini hated judging singers and made no secret of it, but he finally agreed to hear this young Neapolitan. When Caruso came in, Puccini said, "Chi è lei?" ("Who are you?"). The tenor fell right into character and started answering with some of the lines from Rodolfo's first-act narrative, "Che gelida manina": "Chi son? Sono un poeta . . ." ("Who am I? I am a poet . . ."). Caruso got the recommendation and the part.

Emma Eames started putting her foot down as soon as her career began, with no thought of job security. She almost threw away one of her earliest opportunities because she categorically refused to wear the traditional blonde wig while singing Elsa. The argument was finally resolved in her favor when she told the management that if a blonde wig were absolutely necessary for the audience to enjoy *Lohengrin* she would carry the damned thing in on a pole.

One of the great prima donnas of Rudolf Bing's regime and earlier at the Metropolitan is a delightful lady with a gorgeous voice, a sense of humor, and this typically healthy appreciation of her own worth. After a particularly impressive performance as Leonora in Verdi's *Il Trovatore* on tour, she was surrounded by the usual large crowd of admirers. One of them, a writer rather proud of his command of his mother tongue, said, when his turn came, "Madame, tonight your voice sounded like liquid silver."

"Silver," replied the diva in her rich accent, "yes. Others would have said, perhaps, gold. Next!"

On another occasion she was less inclined to correct. When informed by a devotee that she had a voice of velvet, she said, "Velvet. Yes, that is right, velvet."

During an earlier part of this prima donna's stay at the Met it was the custom of the management to have all the young artists who aspired to someday sing leading roles turn out at all the general rehearsals to observe the stars at work. One afternoon the star swept onto the stage fully costumed for a run-through of Ponchielli's *La Gioconda*. She stopped and peered into the darkened auditorium. "And where are all the little Giocondas?" she said. A half dozen of them were there, sitting in a row. "Ah, there you are. Well, listen, listen, listen and learn, learn, learn!"

Everybody's favorite story about this well-loved artist seems to be about the time she was singing *Il Trovatore* at the Metropolitan. The first scene, in which the heroine does not appear, was well under way and her entrance cue was getting more imminent, but she had not yet emerged from her dressing room. An assistant stage manager went dashing to call her again. He knocked on her door and called, "Madame, they are waiting!"

The door opened, and she came out with a beatific smile. "Yes," she said, beaming. "They have no choice."

There is a considerable body of informed opinion which holds that tenors rather than sopranos are as a group most aware of their own central location in the cosmic scheme, and considerable evidence can be adduced to support this contention. It is certain, for example, that during one of the Met tours in the Caruso era somebody tacked a sign on a train compartment reading "Reserved For First Tenor," and it practically precipitated a riot.

One of Colonel Mapleson's tenors in the 1880's, Fancelli, was particularly sure of his own importance. He was not the most astute of men; he once told Mapleson in all seriousness that he realized he needed musical training, but he couldn't spare the time right then. His stated intention was to wait until he retired, when he would have plenty of leisure. At any rate, things went along pretty smoothly for Fancelli until one day he saw a poster advertising the tenor Italo Campanini, following whose name were the words "PRIMO TENORE ASSOLUTO." Fancelli, who could read a little, was infuriated. The word "assoluto" especially got him, and he attacked the poster with a cane in a generally fruitless endeavor to rub it out.

Ultimately Mapleson's company moved on, leaving the offending billboard behind, but the memory kept rankling. Fancelli, as noted, could read a little, but his writing left a lot to be desired. Accordingly he had hired a personal scribe whose chief duty it was to answer the mail and sign Fancelli's "autographs," which were of course never given in public. Invariably his name would be followed by "Primo Tenore Assoluto." The time inevitably came when Fancelli was caught with his scribe down. After a guest appearance he found himself suddenly face-to-face with the Liverpool Philharmonic Society's album, a pen in his hand. Clearly something was expected of him, and he rose bravely to the occasion. With gritted teeth he carefully set down his name, leaving out only one L and the C, followed by the words "Primo Tenore," which he had painstakingly committed to memory. Blinded with success, he ventured forth upon the word "Assoluto." He got the capital A, then three S's before he realized with panic the impossible situation in which he now found himself. There was no way out except by daring frontal attack. He upset the ink-stand over the page, got ink into his hair, and exited amidst the confusion. When the ink dried, the final S had been obliterated. What was left for the eyes of posterity was:

Faneli Primo Tenore Ass

The pride of the prima donna can take many forms, including simple defiance of authority. After Richard Wagner's death his wife Cosima ruled Bayreuth with an iron and sometimes captious hand, and only the strongest-willed personalities ever challenged her. Among them was the indomitable Lilli Lehmann, who appeared as Brünnhilde under Cosima's direction only once despite her acknowledged world-wide supremacy in the role. On that one occasion she chose to wear a bright red wig.

Emma Eames flatly turned down Frau Wagner's request to appear in the 1900 Festival, and made it a point to tell her that she was not willing to submit to the rudeness she had shown artists in the past. She, Eames, did not need that badly either the bigger fees or greater prestige Bayreuth appearances were supposed to mean back in America. When you consider the almost reverent awe in which Bayreuth was held in 1900, Eames' stand is especially noteworthy.

Of course, Cosima Wagner was not the only impresario to feel the wrath of the prima donna. The bigger the stars, the larger the quarrels they were apt to pick with those who would discipline them. Nellie Melba made no secret of her dislike of the Metropolitan management because they dared ask her to be present at rehearsals, and even presumed to tell her what roles they wanted her to sing and where. Her love for Oscar Hammerstein's Manhattan Opera Company was, conversely, founded upon the solid rock of laissez-faire. In her autobiography she tells matter-of-factly of her objections to the Met's necessarily authoritarian approach, complaining bitterly that no artist can give her best when her roles and schedule are dictated by management. She was *Melba*, she claimed, and she would sing when and where she pleased.

Johanna Gadski was another who walked out in protest at managerial authority, although she returned a few seasons later. One year after Heinrich Conried had assumed the reins of the Met from Grau, Gadski stormed out of the company, saying, "Vocal artists cannot be bullied, driven or whipped into getting around for 8 A.M. rehearsals like the little German actors of Conried's little German theatre." Conried, for the record, may have been a man of principle but was not considered a martinet. Except by Gadski.

The mightiest of the stars have even upon occasion taken this high-handed attitude about the very works in which they sing. The great tenor and dynasty-builder Manuel García, father and teacher of Maria Malibran and Pauline Viardot-García, in Naples was once given a role in a new opera he didn't like. Throughout rehearsals he steadfastly refused to sing a note; at dress rehearsal, when worried inquiries were made as to what he would do in performance, he said, "Let the prompter give the words—I'll see to the rest." See to it he did: at the performance he sang the correct text to *his own melodies* while the orchestra played the composer's original accompaniment.

While García's feat may seem like a long way to go to prove a point, at least he was on home ground. Opera stars tend to behave like opera stars wherever they happen to be. Mary Garden was hired to make a silent movie out of the opera *Thaïs* in the days when Fort Lee, New Jersey, was the film capital of the world. She sat quietly while the director, a professional motion picture man, gave her detailed instructions on how he wanted a particular scene played. When he was all through, Garden said, "Thank you; now I will show you how I am going to do it!"

If legitimate authority can rouse this sort of reaction, it is nothing next to the Olympian wrath inspired in the heart of the prima donna by petty officiousness. The folklore of opera bristles with examples of the stars left standing in the rain (or sleet or lava flow) because the doorman didn't recognize them. With the whole performance and an artist's cardiovascular system at stake, somebody arrives to explain things and matters are set right. Usually something clever is said by one of the people involved, although never by the doorman. You can pick from dozens of case histories that fit this general description, but about as well-documented as any is the one involving Melba.

Dame Nellie was singing at the Metropolitan that season. One snowy Sunday she decided to use the canopied front doors rather than the unprotected artist's entrance. The gatekeeper asked her for a ticket. She smiled at him and continued on her way. He stopped her again; nobody got through his post without a ticket. Her smile became a little hard as she explained through clenched teeth that she was Madame Melba. The doorman couldn't have cared less if she had announced she was the Queen of Sheba. He had a simple job, but it was an important one, and by golly he was going to do it right. He kept doing it right as the diva got angrier and angrier. The timely arrival of the manager, Henry Abbey, prevented a disastrous evening and the possibility of some first-rate Australian pyrotechnics. Nonetheless, Melba remained sufficiently close to the incendiary point to demand that Abbey send for the doorman and make him apologize to her, which he did. By the time the contrite gentleman appeared Dame Nellie's wrath had cooled down some, but she still told him that he ought to go down on his knees and beg her forgiveness. He didn't quite go that far, but his humble attitude softened the imperious Melba heart and she let him off with a warning. She later reported, in a self-satisfied way, that he became one of her most loyal servants. A queen was a queen, in those non-unionized days.

For all of Melba's egotism, she at least had the redeeming feature shared by most of her important colleagues: when she failed at something, she could be absolutely candid about it. Like all greats, she could afford to be. One of those failures, the worst of her career, came in December of 1896 at the Met. Against all responsible advice she had determined to sing Brünnhilde in *Siegfried,* one of the heaviest roles in the Wagnerian repertoire. Melba, remember, was a true lyric whose greatest successes were earned in light roles calling for a great deal of coloratura facility. At any rate, the appointed evening began (it also marked Jean and Edouard de Reszke's first local Siegfried and Wanderer). Brünnhilde does not appear until Act III, and to the soprano the first two acts can seem interminable. They were especially so this night as Dame Nellie listened to the huge sounds welling up from the orchestra pit and began to get more and more nervous. Her big scene opens with the warrior-maiden in an enchanted sleep atop a mountain, and as she lay there waiting for de Reszke to come and wake her up the certainty of imminent disaster filled her. She was right. It was brutal. She strained to be heard, her acting style was all wrong, her voice could not have been more out of place. Despite all the help her colleagues gave her, it was a monumental bomb. She tried hard, giving so much that she had to cancel a good part of the rest of her year's engagement to recover, but it was a losing cause. When the final curtain mercifully descended, Melba swept to her dressing room and summoned her manager to admit defeat with a frankness worthy of a prima donna.

"Tell the critics that I am never going to do that again," she said. "It is beyond me. I have been a fool."

Sometimes, of course, enlightened self-interest can encourage candor. Early in her career, Adelina Patti sang for Rossini at his home. The composer was infuriated by the elaborate embellishments she tacked onto the aria "Una voce poco fa" from his *Barber of Seville;* she even had the audacity to change the recitative. When it was finished he smiled coldly and asked, "Who was the composer of the aria you have just sung to us?"

Patti, who was never noted later in her career for her even temper, was wise enough and young enough to want the influential Rossini on her side. It took a little while, but she managed to swallow her pride, apologize, and ask the composer's advice.

Not always are shortcomings on the part of prima donnas admitted and open, of course. After all, the essence of theatre is illusion. For some time before her tragically early death the glamorous Grace Moore had some qualms about her very top notes. In Act II of Puccini's *Tosca* the heroine sings an offstage cantata which mounts to a high C, and these climactic notes Moore had arranged for the fine comprimario Thelma Votipka to sing. It's a not uncommon device, still in use in this work and elsewhere, at every opera house in the world. Management was aware of it, and so were a few of the New York critics, but generally it was a well-kept secret. The inevitable day came, however, when one of the critics mentioned it, and Moore was furious. She at first even accused the utterly reliable (and still blessedly active) "Tippy" of giving away the secret, but it all calmed down soon enough with Moore's reputation emerging more-or-less intact.

Operatic artists are necessarily deeply conscious of success and failure, especially as reflected in the eyes of others. Some, though, have an almost mystical belief in their own talent and either are born with or acquire the ability to sail blithely past all adverse criticism. Victor Maurel, the distinguished

French baritone who was Verdi's original Falstaff and Iago, was such a one. When he read Verdi's published letters, which contained some high praise of him and a few comments not quite so laudatory, he insisted that "there are some things in this book that Verdi never wrote."

More typical, however, was Maestro Arturo Toscanini. He was acutely aware of the distant possibility of perfection, and its elusiveness (more than any critical or public coolness) would make him despair. Once, when he was conducting at La Scala in Milan, he returned home from the theatre to find his family waiting as usual to share his late supper. As they all headed hungrily for the dining room the Maestro blocked their path. "What!" he shouted, "you can eat after such a performance? Shame on you! Shame!" Everybody went to bed hungry.

The images of themselves cherished by both Maurel and Toscanini, though different from each other, have nevertheless a common root with the way most operatic luminaries see themselves. Most of the giants feel that they *are*, somehow, a little different from mortal man. And perhaps they are. It would be hard picturing anybody but a prima donna behaving as Olive Fremstad did during the San Francisco earthquake. When the tremors began and her hotel was being evacuated, she sent a porter back to her suite to fetch a bunch of long-stemmed roses left over from the previous night's *Carmen*. She then sat in the park opposite the hotel and gave them out, one at a time, to the refugees.

Sometimes the image slips a little. When Dame Nellie Melba, by this time of the haut monde, was recording one day she stepped back from the acoustical trumpet after a flawless performance and jammed her posterior into the corner of a table. A clearly produced but unladylike "DAMN!" resulted, and when the record was played back the "damn" was preserved beautifully, but not, alas, for posterity. The recording was remade after the table had been moved.

Opera composers, though a proud lot, generally have left the wilder reaches of temperament to the performers. When they have expressed themselves in this direction it's usually in comparatively private circumstances. Thus, Richard Strauss' comment after hearing some works by Frederick Delius, the English composer—"I had no idea that anyone except myself was writing such good music"—was not originally intended for public consumption, any more than was Delius' after hearing a few of his own English songs sung by a garble-tongued English baritone—"Admirable, but what language was he singing in?"

As a matter of fact, the composer often shelters his pride behind a gentle sort of self-effacement. Giacomo Puccini made such severe demands upon his librettist, Luigi Illica, that he would send along contrite little gifts of food to placate him. He wrote in a letter: "Forgive me for the mental anguish which must come with my letters. As for the gastronomical anguish . . . this will come with my cooking."

Claude Debussy had a wry awareness of reality. After the success of his *Pelléas et Mélisande* he had sold the rights to first productions of all subsequent operas (among which was supposed to be one based on Poe's *The Fall of the House of Usher*) to Giulio Gatti-Casazza, then the General Manager of the Metropolitan. Time passed, and of course Debussy never got around to writing any other operas; he even started doubting his ability to do so. "The man for the public," he told Gatti in one of the series of talks they had on the matter, "is that amazing Puccini." As Debussy knew, "that amazing Puccini" had tried to secure Maeterlinck's play *Pelléas et Mélisande* for his own use, only to discover the rights had already been purchased.

Gatti tried to cheer the composer. "Your genius," he said, "is très aristocratique."

"Très aristocratique?" Debussy smiled sadly. "*Trop* aristocratique."

Although Illica's fame rests chiefly on his collaborations with Puccini, he wrote many libretti for other composers. *Tosca,* one of his most successful, was originally adapted from the Sardou original not for Puccini, but for Alberto Franchetti. Franchetti worked on it for a while, then returned it to Illica, telling him it was unmusical. The argument that automatically ensued grew increasingly bitter, until finally Franchetti persuaded Giuseppe Verdi, the revered Grand Master of Italian opera, to sit as arbitrator. The day of the judgment approached, and Illica read his script aloud to Verdi and Franchetti. There was silence until after he had read the words to what later became the tenor's lovely third-act aria "E lucevan le stelle"; then the old Maestro leaped to his feet and shouted, "Bravo! Bellissimo! Ma bravo Illica."

The dumbfounded Franchetti became even more upset when Verdi turned on him and started berating him for not knowing a good libretto when he read one, for demanding far more than he, Verdi, had ever dreamed of having until his last years. The young composer stammered out a few bewildered questions: how would the Maestro set "E lucevan," as an arioso, a recitative, a romanza . . . what?

"My dear Franchetti," the old genius replied, "I would simply make some music, a little music, that's all."

The little music, of course, was ultimately supplied by Puccini.

Verdi's relationship to *Tosca* didn't quite end there. His friend, the acerbic conductor Leopoldo Mugnone, delighted in telling about Verdi and the *Tosca* bells. It seems that one day the composer asked Mugnone how come he was traveling so often to nearby Pistoia.

"Why, Maestro, I go there to supervise the casting of the bells for *Tosca,* Puccini's new opera, which will be given this winter and which I shall conduct."

"What? Bells in *Tosca*? How many bells? And what are they used for?"

"They will be used in Act III, which pictures the awakening of Rome with the chimes of the various churches, and there are eleven of them."

The old composer turned away, muttering as he left, "Eleven! Eleven! It seems incredible."

A number of days passed before the two men again met. Verdi asked, "How are your eleven bells getting along, my dear Mugnone? I believe there are eleven—am I right?"

"They are coming along well, and there are really eleven of them."

Verdi shook his head. "And to think that when I composed *Il Trovatore* I was so much perplexed as to whether or not I should introduce that one poor bell in the Miserere! It seemed to me all the impresarios of the time would hurl their curses at me. The world has progressed." And the old man stumped sadly away.

The classic story of this genre is, unfortunately, apocryphal. For the record, though, here it is: Rossini and Donizetti were attending a lavish party during the course of which the hostess gave them manuscript paper and asked both guests to compose a short piece. Rossini and Donizetti turned in a few identical measures: the same tune, rhythm, everything. The hostess was triumphant.

"You see," she cried, "it is possible for two great creative talents to arrive independently at the same result."

"Not at all, Madame," Donizetti replied; "we both stole it from Bellini."

Chapter 8

Not Quite as Written

THE PRODUCTION OF OPERA is an exquisitely balanced intertwining of myriads of details. Cast, chorus, orchestra, ballet, sets, supers, costumes, props, backstage machinery, special effects and simple human cussedness all spiral into an incredibly complex undertaking the wonder of which is that it ever succeeds at all. There are a bewildering number of opportunities for disaster to strike somewhere along the line. And strike it sometimes does. Many of the most treasurable moments in operatic history are the results of a momentary breakdown in the awesome smoothness of the usual operating procedures.

Sometimes, of course, accidents are a great deal less than funny, as when a piece of scenery fell on Giorgio Tozzi's head during a Metropolitan presentation of Mozart's *The Magic Flute*. As the priest-king, Sarastro, the basso was wearing a substantial wig, which may have prevented drastic injury, but even so he completed the performance, and indeed spent the rest of the week with a monstrous headache. Most of the time, though, there seems to be a special providence that watches over singers, even tall ones, so that on-the-job mutilations are at a surprising minimum considering the hazards. Most operatic catastrophes are occasions for hilarity rather than first aid.

When accidents do happen, it's usually better to ignore them, leaving bad enough alone, as it were. Attempts at rectification, no matter how well-meaning, invariably seem to compound the idiocy of the situation. One evening when the gifted American baritone Robert Merrill was singing Amonasro in *Aida* he set off across the stage without realizing that the large soprano with whom he was performing was standing on his sandal. With his first step the strap broke. Using admirable presence of mind, he managed to kick the shoe off and into the orchestra pit. All would have been well if one of the solicitous musicians hadn't tossed the sandal back onto the stage.

In the passion of performance dramatic enthusiasm can lead to unexpected difficulties. On one notable occasion, Clara Louise Kellogg, playing Leonora, interposed in the duel between Manrico and De Luna in Act I of *Il Trovatore*, as per the stage directions. The tenor was a husky brute, and Kellogg, carried away by the drama, leaned heavily on his massive shoulder. Manrico was totally unprepared for this flank assault, however, and was thrown so precipitously off-balance that he fell flat on his face. Kellogg, who had been depending on his apparently rock-like form to support her, collapsed on top of him. De Luna was left waving his sword at a slowly rising dust cloud in what was surely the most ignominious conclusion to any duel he had ever fought.

Even moments of dignity and grandeur have fallen victim to the overeager prima donna. It must have been extremely difficult to get an audience back into the proper mood at a performance of *Norma* in which the great Titiens, as the Druid priestess, preparing to sound the huge gong, drew her drumstick back so hard she hit her tenor Giuglini a wicked smash on the nose. The ensuing nosebleed caused considerable consternation, particularly on the part of the wounded man.

Recalcitrant sound effects and stage props have been responsible for more unintended laughter than any other single factor, again more often than not intensified by confused remedial efforts. Verdi's *La Forza del Destino* has a libretto founded almost completely on the workings of coincidence. The climax of the first scene comes when the hero, Don Alvaro, throws down his pistol in surrender only to have it accidentally go off and kill the father of his beloved. Normally there is a stagehand hidden under a table nearby clutching a revolver loaded with blanks, ready to fire on cue. Enrico Caruso was singing Alvaro on a memorable night when he threw his pistol to the floor—and there was no shot. The singers on stage looked at each other despairingly for a moment, until Caruso triumphantly shouted, "BANG!"

(Taking her cue from this famous story, a soprano singing in *La Traviata* at the New York City Opera recently couldn't find the bell with which she was to summon her maid, so she waved her hand in the air and delicately called, "ting-a-ling.")

Forza provided Beniamino Gigli with some of the most harrowing moments of his sparkling career. His gun, like Caruso's, didn't "fire" in the opening scene, the prop man, snug under his table, having fallen asleep. Unlike his great predecessor, Gigli ignored the silence and he and his colleagues continued the scene. He was despairing over the corpse of Leonora's father when, at least thirty seconds too late, some eager genius backstage found a pistol and shot it. The delayed explosion terrified the cast and broke up the audience. From that point on, the performance was doomed to recurrent fits of mirth.

In Act II, the wounded Alvaro was being carried on a stretcher when one of the stretcher-bearers tripped and dropped his handles, sending Gigli rolling off onto the floor. The tenor had to get up amidst the howls of laughter and climb back. Finally, in what might have been a shattering conclusion to a strange evening but for a curtaining monk's robe, Gigli bent down to pick up a sword for his fourth-act duel with Don Carlo and his breeches split all the way up the back. Obviously, the willingness to persist in the face of adversity is a useful accessory to vocal talent.

Gigli, as a matter of fact, was probably more self-possessed than most singers. Few things threw him off his stride. While he was singing "Che gelida manina" in Act I of a *La Bohème* at Covent Garden, the small pot-bellied stove on stage caught fire. He calmly tried to douse the blaze with the contents of a small bottle of water that happened to be nearby, but it did no good. Still singing, he walked to the wings where some minor functionaries were jumping up and down. "Please fire, please fire, please fire," he sang with the music, whereupon he was handed a bucket of water. He dumped it on the conflagration that was still cheerfully raging on stage, making a few more trips until, during the soprano's aria "Si, mi chiamano Mimi" he finally had it extinguished. Just in time for the big duet, by the way.

It's hard to pinpoint the reason, but Wagner's music-dramas have always seemed the most accident-prone. Perhaps it's because they call for so much in the way of spectacular mechanical effects like Magic Fire and descents into Nibelheim and the docking of boats, or perhaps it's because they tend to take themselves so seriously that lapses from perfection are all the more noticeable. Regardless, some of the choicest gems of risible calamity were born amidst the spears and helmets of the Wagnerian wing.

Sometimes the difficulties would come in an epidemic. The Metropolitan season of 1899 was plagued by a rash of anvil trouble in *Siegfried*. In the first act, the young hero is supposed to try out his newly-forged sword by slamming it into his anvil, which thereupon slices in two like a piece of cheese. It's a very effective climax to the scene, except that throughout this ill-starred season the pre-rigged anvil kept falling into two halves a second or so before Siegfried hit it, leaving the skin-clad tenor with sword upraised and egg on his face. Stage crews would labor over the thing between performances, it would work fine in rehearsal, and then with imbecile precision it would divide itself like the Red Sea as soon as Siegfried lifted his arm. A very distressing manifestation, indeed, and one that ended of its own accord by the next time the opera was in the repertoire.

That Magic Fire mentioned a moment ago is a tricky thing

to manage. Brünnhilde, put to enchanted sleep by her father, the god Wotan, is surrounded by a ring of flames atop her mountain as *Die Walküre* ends. When it works properly the impact is very powerful, and to make it work properly, stage designers have used a vast arsenal of devices from steam jets to smoke bombs to colored cellophane to complicated projection systems. Usually it all works best in the large permanent opera companies or specialized theatres like Bayreuth, where they are equipped to handle demands like this. In outlying communities, though, makeshift methods have often led to ruin. Olive Fremstad was reclining on her rock at the end of a *Walküre* in St. Louis when she suddenly realized that she was perilously close to choking. The smoke of the Magic Fire appeared to be real smoke, not steam at all, and what's more it smelled particularly vile. She lay still as long as she dared, then called out loudly to her secretary in the wings, "Go at once and tell them that if they don't shut off this stink, I shall get up and walk away right before the public!" Inasmuch as much of the public had heard her make the threat anyway, the actual walking out would have been hardly more devastating to the mood of the remarkably moving scene, which blessedly soon ended, stink and all.

Lohengrin provided opera with one of its most oft-repeated quotes. Leo Slezak, the great Viennese tenor, was singing the title part when, in Act III, he discovered that the Swan-boat in which he was supposed to exit had been towed off without him. Turning to a member of the chorus standing nearby, he asked, "When does the next swan leave?"

It was precisely this sort of sang-froid that deserted Christine Nilsson when she sang Elsa in *Lohengrin* during the 1880 London season. Somehow she completely lost her way in the middle of the Act II duet with Ortrud, which struck her as uproariously funny. She got a bad case of the giggles, so bad that she had to turn upstage, shaking helplessly with laughter. She never even tried to pick up her music until Lohengrin's entrance, leaving poor Ortrud to fend for herself.

David Bispham, the American baritone, was singing Telramund in this same opera in Baltimore around the turn of the century when he had his concentration ruined early. In Act I, at the approach of the Swan-knight, Telramund hurls defiance at him, and the chorus is then supposed to open up the half-circle in which it has been grouped, thus allowing Lohengrin to come in on his boat. Bispham's defiance got hurled just fine, and the chorus realigned itself on cue, but instead of a back-drop showing the banks of the river Scheldt near medieval Antwerp there was revealed a huge painted Thames River, complete with boats and boathouses, all decked out for the Henley Regatta. It was a little difficult to continue.

Bispham was involved in another traumatic evening with Richard Wagner. The date was May 23, 1899, and the work was *The Flying Dutchman* starring himself and Johanna Gadski. Prior to the curtain he had had an opportunity to examine the Dutchman's ship, which was so rickety and moth-eaten he felt a premonition of the disaster that was soon to overtake him. At his first entrance he was a little appalled by the canvas "ocean," which was set into stormy waves by a flock of little boys crawling around underneath while a crew of men flapped canvas streamers in the air, but it all seemed dreadfully insignificant when he felt the first lurch of his ship as it headed uncertainly towards shore riding on six iron wheels and propelled by four burly stage-hands pushing from below. He managed to keep his balance, albeit a little shakily, while going over his opening scene in his mind: the ship will beach, he will leap ashore and begin the powerful monologue "Die frist ist um" telling of how his latest seven-year term of wandering was now over . . . except this evening it was not to be. The stagehands pushed the ship creakily onto the stage and executed a graceful turn, but just before it was about to land the wheels got stuck in a big crack on the stage floor. With about eight feet left to go, the ship stopped dead. It heaved and shuddered as the men pushed it, but there it stayed, too far away from shore for Bispham to jump yet close enough to be in full view of the entire audience. There was nothing to do but sweat it out while hoping for the best, especially as the monologue made precious little sense sung from on board a ship that had not yet landed.

The cue came for the Dutchman to sing. Karl Muck, the conductor, looked at Bispham. Bispham stared stolidly ahead without moving, a resigned expression on his face. Muck started chortling happily at the situation, which got the orchestra players up on their feet to see what was happening. They were treated to the sight of the ship shuddering violently, its masts waving back and forth, as its stern lifted a full foot in the air and then crashed loudly down. There were a few titters in the audience, but they were quickly shushed by the Wagner worshipers to whom, especially in 1899, the Master's works were akin to holy writ. In the silence that now settled on Covent Garden, groans and straining could be heard from somewhere deep down in the painted ocean. Finally a loud clear voice emanating from the bowels of the ship broke the stillness. It said, "Why don't you shove 'er along, Bill?"

"'Ow can I," Bill answered reasonably, "when the blasted thing is stuck fast in the styge?"

This did it for even the staunchest devotees. The audience burst into laughter, with Bispham, clutching onto a mast of his cavorting vessel for dear life, trying desperately to keep a straight face. The performance seemed as if it might never get going again, what with the star unable to get ashore. To the rescue, however, came the head carpenter. He was wearing a derby hat and carried over his head a ten-foot wooden plank. With the hat and the lumber showing above the "water," he "waded" out to the stranded ship, placing one end of the plank near Bispham and the other on the rocks. Then he tipped his hat, saying in a clear voice, "Now you can get off, sir," and "waded" off stage. Bispham somehow managed to stagger across the narrow board, and sang.

His hour of trial was not yet over, though. There was still Act III, wherein the Dutchman reboards his ship and bitterly sails away. With trepidation Bispham got on board and cast off. Sure enough, the ship slid a few inches from shore and then ground to a halt, stuck tight in another crack. Gadski, who as Senta was supposed to throw herself into the sea to redeem the Dutchman, had to squeeze down between the boat and the rocks as best she could. As she slowly climbed down out of sight one of the prop men, oblivious to everything except the instructions he had been given, tossed a glass-full of water onto the stage to represent the splash of Senta's falling body. In a final burst of ill-advised realism, one of the supers on stage crowned the entire lunatic affair by throwing out a life-preserver.

With Gadski jammed inextricably somewhere in the scenery and Bispham stranded on his immobile ship, Covent Garden had to fall back upon its pre-arranged plan whereby in emergencies a substitute Dutchman and Senta would be hauled up to heaven during the transfiguration scene that climaxes the opera. Unfortunately, to the joint dismay of both Gadski and Bispham, instead of a pair of supers costumed and made up to look like them, two twelve-year-old street urchins rose jerkily from amidst the flapping canvas waves and ascended to salvation clutching each other fearfully. It was a fitting end to a noteworthy night.

Sir Thomas Beecham, who was usually prepared for anything, found himself caught unawares when, in his 1912 tour of the provinces, the curtain suddenly came down in the middle of the third act of *Die Meistersinger*. He frantically pushed the little button near the podium that was supposed to ring the signal-bell controlling this sort of thing, and after a moment the curtain rose again. Before Beecham had time to complete his sigh of relief, though, the curtain slammed shut once more. Again the bell was rung, even more urgently, and again the curtain rose, this time staying up until the end of the music. Sir Thomas, who had completed conducting with one eye cocked on the curtain and one hand near the signal-button, tore backstage with murder in his heart, determined to impale his tormentor with a few choice witticisms. The little curtain-puller's explanation, though, was so ingenuous that Beecham's fury completely evaporated. The unfortunate stagehand had been lulled to sleep by Wagner's score and, awakening suddenly, saw that it was after eleven o'clock.

As no opera in his memory had ever gone past that hour, he was certain that he had overslept and missed his cue, so he hastily closed the curtain. The frenzied ringing of his bell had impelled him to raise it again, but as he sat there reflecting on his dear wife waiting for supper he became all the more certain that there was a mistake somewhere. Hence the curtain fell for the second time. The subsequent pealing of his bell convinced him finally to get it up and keep it that way, but his explanation ended with a bitter attack on Sir Thomas for not having brought the opera to a close before eleven P.M., a disgraceful hour at best. Rather than defend Wagner, Beecham just nodded and went away.

Parsifal is of all the Wagnerian canon the most sacrosanct and hence the most susceptible to the humor of incongruity. For quite a while it could not even be played anywhere outside the hallowed confines of Bayreuth, and even today it's treated with a solemnity verging perilously close to pomposity. From there it's an easy step to the preposterous, with the second act, replete with magicians and overstuffed Flower Maidens, as often as not taking the step. It was in that act, during the seduction scene, that Olive Fremstad underwent one of the more trying sequences of her career. She was busily trying to win the affections of Parsifal, played by Karl Jörn, when an overhead scaffolding gave way. Into view, clutching for dear life to the askew planking, came the pair of stagehands who were supposed to strew the lovers with blossoms. Embarrassed by this sudden descent to public examination, they climbed and crawled back and forth on the scaffold, slipping and sliding, while Parsifal roared with laughter and Kundry alternately cried and scolded them loudly. The men were safely pulled back up into the accustomed anonymity of the fly space just barely in time to keep the presentation from disintegrating into chaos.

This same scene almost proved the undoing of the Belgian dramatic tenor Ernest Van Dyck when he sang the title role at Bayreuth with Materna as Kundry during the last decade of the Nineteenth Century. In the middle of the love-making he stepped too far back and his flowing golden wig got caught in the branches of the "mystic forest" that surrounded them. At that very instant the cue came for a magical scene change, and the vines and leaves and trees slowly began to rise, bearing with them Van Dyck's wig. As it lifted majestically off his head it revealed his shiny bald pate to the fascinated audience. The distraught tenor leaped high into the air, managing to knock the toupee free of the branches a split second before it sailed completely out of reach. It fell to the stage and as he stooped down to get it he heard the music for his next line, which completely panicked him. He swept the wig off the floor, slamming it onto his head as he began to sing. Unfortunately, he got it on backwards, with the long locks dangling in front of his face. As he had his back to the audience, this only accentuated his baldness by outlining his bare scalp with a fringe of gold, but it was even worse when he turned towards the footlights. He looked like Hairless Joe from Al Capp's Dogpatch. Yellow curls completely hid his face with the exception of his nose. By this time the sedate Festival public was in hysterics.

Van Dyck knelt next to the reclining Kundry to sing of his love, and the quick-thinking Materna tenderly stroked where she estimated his forehead to be, thereby parting the mass of hair and allowing him to see and be seen. It was elementary tonsorial repair, but effective for the moment. As soon as Kundry began to sing *her* long passage, Van Dyck bolted to the wings to straighten the cursed toupee more permanently. His anxiety got the better of him, though, and he ripped the offending wig off his head a stride or two early so that the audience was treated to a parting glimpse of his pate, gleaming gloriously in the spotlight.

It's impossible to tell in advance from what quarter operatic misadventure may strike. Indeed, it often seems to dog the heels of the best-prepared. When David Bispham sang *Falstaff* for the first time with the Covent Garden company he put a great deal of thought and effort into devising and affixing his costume and makeup, an elaborate combination of stuffed waistcoats, wig, beard, and putty nose which was, when completed, very impressive. It was not to be Bispham's night, though: it was warm, and the baritone sweated so that his carefully constructed putty nose began slowly to elongate until he looked like a freakish Cyrano. His surreptitious efforts towards rebuilding were to no avail. Finally the nose gave up completely and slid damply to the floor. Bispham, his view obstructed by his enormous padded belly, couldn't see where the piece of putty had fallen. The final touch has something of the inevitability of Greek drama: he stepped on the putty, skidded, and fell flat on his padded rear end.

Among the most successful of Sir Thomas Beecham's ventures as a producer of opera were his presentations at Covent Garden of Strauss' *Elektra* in 1910 and *Salome* in 1911. Both had their share of trouble, although *Elektra* got through comparatively unscathed. Beecham did remember one night, in which he had intended participating only as a spectator, when the two messengers, who are supposed to appear midway through, sing a little and then dash out, suddenly reappeared about five minutes later and went through their scene again. Beecham rubbed his eyes, then leaned over to Albert Sammons, the conductor.

"Have those two fellows been here before?"

"Yes."

"Are you certain?"

"There is no doubt about it."

Inasmuch as the leader of the second violins corroborated his conductor's opinion, Beecham stomped backstage to find out what the hell was going on. Investigation revealed that the messengers had been sent back on by the chorus master, who had missed their first entrance because he was occupied in kicking an unruly chorister out the stage door. He had heard some vaguely familiar musical phrases, seen the two messengers standing nearby, and directed them to make their entrance despite their protestations of having already done so. Rather than argue with the chorus master the pair went back on stage, repeating their lines at the first appropriate moment and then beating a hasty retreat. Beecham let the whole thing drop when he realized that nobody in the audience had noticed.

Sir Thomas' troubles with *Salome* were a little more complex. After the success of *Elektra* it seemed only natural to premiere the earlier opera, especially as he was fortunate enough to have an option on the services of the soprano Aino Akte, but the censors forbade it. Beecham appealed directly to Prime Minister Asquith, as a result of which a meeting was set up at St. James' Palace between Sir Thomas on one side and the Lord Chamberlain and his assistant on the other. Beecham was informed that one of the key objections was the public outcry against showing a Biblical figure, John the Baptist, on the stage; *Samson* was another matter, that being Old Testament. The debate got pretty theological for a while, but the upshot of it all was that Beecham could after all present *Salome*, providing he consent to a few minor changes.

The "few minor changes" involved such drastic surgery as changing John's name to just "the Prophet"; bowdlerizing all the passages between him and Salome; changing her lust for his body to a desire for spiritual guidance; altering her line at the end from "if you would have looked upon me you would have loved me" to ". . . you would have blessed me"—in short, the entire piece was transformed into what Beecham called a "comforting sermon." Still, there was nothing he could do but turn the castrated libretto over to be re-translated into German and handed out to the cast to learn.

The singers, as may be imagined, were somewhat less than overjoyed at the changes. As a matter of fact, they fought bitterly, with some of the quarrels even breaking out into print, but in the end they gave way to Beecham's firm stand: it was *Salome* this way or not at all. Throughout the rehearsal period things kept cropping up. For example, what were they to do about the severed head of John the Baptist that is supposed to be shown at the end? The Lord Chamberlain's office suggested that Miss Akte sing the last scene to a bloody sword, but she demurred on the grounds that it might ruin her dress. The compromise that was reached called for a tray to be brought on stage covered with a cloth without even the suggestion of a bulge.

With much pain the opening performance finally came. A huge throng jammed the theatre, whipped to feverish excitement by the unremitting rash of articles in the press playing up the more sensational aspects of the opera and detailing Beecham's troubles with the censors. Despite Sir Thomas' anxiety, the performance started out very tamely. Then suddenly Salome slipped back into the original version for a line or two. The audience didn't seem to notice, but Beecham was jolted as if he had grabbed a bare wire. He listened breathlessly for a while, and for a while the censored version was used, but little by little, as the excitement of the performance gripped them, the cast all lapsed into the original text. Beecham was terrified. Out front, amidst the many dignitaries, sat the Prime Minister and the Lord Chamberlain. He tried as hard as he could to make the orchestra play loudly enough to drown out the singers, but it was no use. Every word of the performance seemed to him to emerge with crystalline clarity and, judging from the ovation at the end, shattering effect.

Beecham dreaded the inevitable backstage meeting with the Lord Chamberlain's party, certain that this spelled the end of his career. His astonishment was all the greater, then, when the Lord Chamberlain approached him beaming, hand outstretched. "It has been wonderful," he said; "we are all delighted and I felt I could not leave the theatre without thanking you and your colleagues for the complete way in which you have met and fulfilled all our wishes."

To the day he died Sir Thomas didn't know whether to thank the poor diction of his cast or the poor German of the Lord Chamberlain.

Interruptions from outside sources have hilariously broken up many an opera. One of the more common types involves the children of prima donnas who, on seeing their mothers in all sorts of dreadful situations down there on the stage, give vent to their natural feelings at the top of their lungs. There are many stories of this kind, but one will suffice to illustrate the point: When Ernestine Schumann-Heink took her kids to see her play the Witch in *Hansel and Gretel* she forgot to brief them on what to expect, so that when she was pushed into the oven one of her little boys yelled, "Oh! They're throwing my mother in the oven and burning her up!" Despite assurances from some of his more sophisticated siblings he kept crying and calling "MOTHER!" as loudly as he could. When she finally emerged unscathed he shouted delightedly, "They didn't burn her up!" Schumann-Heink, a warm and loving person as well as a superlative artist, was entranced by the whole episode.

Total strangers can be even more disruptive than children. At a provincial performance of *Aida* by a small company touring the South, things progressed rather well until the Nile Scene. At a dramatic moment the soprano tried to lean on a tree, but her pressure was interpreted by somebody backstage to mean that the scene was over and the whole backdrop was summarily lifted up into the fly space, revealing the brick wall at the back of the stage to the wondering audience. The singers kept going with admirable aplomb, but worse was yet to come. At the very rear of the stage, in an area normally hidden from view by scenery, a door opened and a small delivery boy wearing a white coat and carrying what looked like a lunch order started tiptoeing across the stage. He had gotten halfway to the other side when he realized something was wrong and stopped dead still. Slowly he turned until he was facing the audience. His eyes widening with terror, he dropped the lunch, and said "Oh my God!" and dashed back the way he had come. As he exited, everybody could read the bright red lettering on the back of his jacket which exhorted them to drink a certain popular soft drink. The Nile Scene had run its course.

Mary Garden in her autobiography tells of seeing a performance of *La Bohème* in a nameless American town that was given in a hall in which on other nights the circus was performing. The animals from the menagerie were housed in the basement. During the first-act love duet a curious giraffe stuck his tongue through a hole in the stage floor, a sight that at first terrified but then convulsed the cast and the conductor.

The same artist was present in Chicago during Gounod's *Roméo et Juliette* when a man dashed up out of the audience and threatened the Roméo, Jean de Reszke, with a gun. De Reszke remained calm while stagehands collared the would-be assassin and dragged him off, then resumed his role as if nothing had happened. The tenor later told Garden that Nellie Melba, who was singing Juliette, "remained behind her shutters on the balcony, screaming like a lunatic. She kept shouting backstage, 'Ring down the curtain! My voice is gone!' And then I lost my temper for the first time and called up to her, 'For God's sake, keep quiet, Melba, and open the windows and come out!'" Melba emerged, and the evening ended triumphantly for both of them.

That Melba should be frightened by a madman waving a gun is not necessarily surprising, although normally she was the most self-controlled of prima donnas. At her tear-laden farewell to Covent Garden in 1926, at which she sang an act of *La Bohème*, she was so overcome by emotion that some stagehands thoughtfully held the curtains closed for her. The diva quickly recovered, ordering them to "pull back those bloody curtains at once!"—a proper conclusion to a noble career.

Opera stars, accustomed to the extraordinary, are often notably adaptable no matter how outré the situation in which they may find themselves, in or out of the theatre. Risë Stevens was en route to a concert with her accompanist when she began noticing the erratic driving of the chauffeur of her rented limousine. A little careful watching soon revealed that he was thoroughly drunk. As Miss Stevens didn't relish the prospect of being driven into a tree, she contrived to ask the plastered driver to stop and get her a hamburger. He grumpily complied, and as soon as he had left his seat the prima donna grabbed the wheel, leaving tire marks behind her in her haste to get away. She arrived at the recital hall in one piece, the concert proceeding as scheduled. At its conclusion the somewhat sobered chauffeur showed up with a covey of police in tow, determined to press auto-theft charges until the cluster of dignitaries surrounding Miss Stevens awed him into changing his mind.

Marjorie Lawrence, who was scheduled to catch a train following a Brünnhilde she sang in St. Louis, found the performance ran so late that she dashed to the station in full costume, helmet and all, only to discover that the train had just pulled out. She frantically hired an automobile to catch up with it at the next station. This time she made it, climbing breathlessly aboard the last car still wearing her warrior-maiden garb. Her spectacular appearance galvanized the passengers, one of whom shouted, "It must be a hold-up!"

A creative demonstration of aplomb was afforded by the renowned Nineteenth-Century basso, Luigi Lablache, when he was singing in London with what came to be known as the "Puritani" quartet, the other members of which were Grisi, Mario (replacing Rubini) and Tamburini. He stayed at a hotel which housed a number of other theatrical personalities including the famous midget, General Tom Thumb. While resting one day, the singer was intruded upon by a frantic English tourist, who apologized, all a-fluster, explaining that he was desperately trying to see Tom Thumb.

"I am he," intoned the extremely tall basso in his deepest voice.

The Englishman stared at him in bewilderment. "But you were much smaller when I saw you on stage yesterday," he said.

Lablache smiled conspiratorially. "Yes, that is how I have to appear, but when I get home to my own rooms I let myself out and enjoy myself."

Natalie Bodanya needed all the sang-froid she could muster when, in a 1937 Metropolitan presentation of Pergolesi's *Il Matrimonio Segreto*, she lost one of her petticoats on stage. She simply kicked it aside as if that sort of thing happened all the time. In an earlier day, Frances Alda was prevented from getting away with a similar maneuver by the prankster proclivities of Enrico Caruso. It was during Act I of *La*

Bohème that she felt the button holding up her pantalettes give way. She quickly slipped behind a handy sofa, where she unobtrusively stepped out of the garment and went on with the music. Caruso, however, had noticed what was going on; not being the man to let an opportunity like this go to waste, he picked up the drawers and spread them out on the sofa while the audience guffawed.

Practical jokes had been a part of opera since long before their most famous practitioner, Caruso, rolled his first spitball, and they are still very much a part of the scene. It was only recently, in San Francisco, that the players in Act II of *La Bohème* were disturbed by the presence on stage of what looked like a gaudily dressed local dowager busily ogling all the men in the cast. It was some time before anybody realized that this odd apparition was actually the fine comprimario tenor, Alessio de Paolis, disguised to the teeth. The trickster is as firmly entrenched in musical history as the prompter.

That same Frances Alda who had underwear trouble in *La Bohème* ran into a different sort of difficulty when she sang Marguerite in Gounod's *Faust* for the first time at the Metropolitan. As she tried to turn her spinning wheel, a most necessary effect, she discovered that somebody had nailed it so that it wouldn't move. After a few futile passes at the stubborn apparatus, she abandoned it and went on with the scene, which proceeded beautifully. In high spirits, she went to her house to make her exit—only to find that somebody had nailed the door shut.

Lotte Lehmann once discovered the futility of trying to get the best of a tenor. She was singing Agathe in Weber's *Der Freischütz* during an outdoor season in the Pine Forest at Zoppot when she made and won a bet with Richard Tauber, who was singing Max. The stakes had been a bar of chocolate, payment of which she demanded one evening shortly before a performance. Tauber told her that she'd get it in due course. Lehmann, underestimating her man, had no idea that by "due course" Tauber meant on stage in the middle of the opera, but that's when she got it; just at the moment Agathe runs ecstatically into Max's arms singing "sweetly enraptured" he handed her a bright silver foil-wrapped candy bar. The startled soprano juggled it around momentarily before depositing it on a bench, where it glistened gaily in the lights. The girl who was singing Aennchen promptly sat on it and refused to move for the rest of the act. Because all three were on the verge of hysterics, they had to sing all evening long without looking at each other.

Practical joking was nothing new to Lehmann. Early in her career, when she was still in Hamburg, she sang in Goldmark's *The Cricket on the Hearth*. In Act II her colleagues solemnly and slowly wound her up in yard after yard of wool until she looked like a cocoon. Not knowing quite what else to do she kept singing her part, ignoring the frantic gestures of the convulsed Elisabeth Schumann who kept signaling from the wings for her to break the strands. Lehmann remembered that it wasn't too bad until the point arrived at which the stage directions told her to stand up.

Melba, of all people, was quite the trickster, although she normally confined her activities to offstage moments. Typical of her activities in this non-musical field was her revenge on the rich playboy, dilettante and sometime composer Herman Bemberg. She was appearing in his opera *Elaine* at Covent Garden, during the rehearsals for which he began to use the prima donna's dressing room as his own private closet, dumping all his belongings there while he went out front to watch, which left precious little space for Melba's things. On the second night of the opera the soprano arrived and found the usual clutter of Bemberg's hat, coat and umbrella strewn across the room and filling the single chair. With great care Melba cut the brim of the hat almost all the way around, leaving it just attached, covered the inside with black grease paint, slit the umbrella so that it would fall apart when opened, and put two eggs in the overcoat pockets. Bemberg, as per his custom, dashed in after the third act, scooped up his belongings and dashed out to join some important friends waiting for him in a box. By all accounts his arrival there was awe-inspiring.

The king of all jokers, of course, was the king of all tenors

Enrico Caruso. He was irrepressible. Some of his on-stage gags have become world-famous, as the time he came out in a highly dramatic scene and handed Antonio Scotti a raw egg. Once, when playing Nemorino in *L'Elisir d'Amore*, one of his most triumphant roles, he decided that the magic elixir didn't look wonderful enough. Unbeknownst to any of his colleagues he slipped a chemical into the jug to make it fizz a little, then shook it up. It fizzed, all right: it practically exploded, drenching not only the tenor but everybody standing nearby.

For some reason, possibly because of the generally high spirits that pervade much of the work, Caruso concentrated a lot of his horseplay on the opera *La Bohème*. One of his earlier tricks was sewing up the sleeves of Colline's coat, which provided many a basso with embarrassing moments after his lovely fourth-act Farewell to the Coat. Once, the basso Arimondi was playing Colline and, naturally suspicious of Caruso, tried the sleeves before putting on the coat. All was well; with a sigh of relief Arimondi slipped into the coat, then put on his top hat—and got doused with water.

One particular performance of *La Bohème* by the Metropolitan in Philadelphia was made almost a shambles by the fun-and-games indulged in by the leads, Caruso, Scotti, Andres de Segurola, and Frances Alda, each of whom was fined one hundred dollars by the management for indulging in the fracas. At Mimi's entrance she found the Bohemians wearing trick monocles in the left eye; as she bent to warm herself someone squirted seltzer in her face; in the Cafe Momus scene she discovered that the waiter was one of her best friends; the "snow" in Act III included paper, string, buttons and nails; de Segurola's hat in Act IV was filled with flour which thickly covered his head and shoulders when he put it on; the prop glass contained ink instead of water; Mimi's bed had two of the casters removed so that it wobbled wildly. All in all, Mimi that night died of the giggles, not TB: Alda was laughing so hard at the end she had to turn her back on the audience.

While singing Rodolfo to Melba's Mimi in Monte Carlo

in 1902 Caruso behaved until Act IV; then, as Dame Nellie lay dying, with her lover hovering sadly near, she kept hearing a little squeaking noise. Every time Caruso leaned solicitously toward her, the squeak would sound again, for all the world as if he had noisy joints. Finally Melba determined—and the realization almost ruined her singing for the night—that he was carefully squeezing a little rubber toy next to her ear while looking increasingly unhappy with each squeak.

These two artists were singing the same roles at Covent Garden when a third party got involved. During Act II when neither of them had too much to sing, Melba suddenly whispered, "For heaven's sake, look at Tosti." Out front, in the first row of the audience, the famous and dignified baritone-composer Paolo Tosti was staring at them goggle-eyed, with cheeks puffed, wearing a white handkerchief as a mustache. For once, it was Caruso who almost broke up.

There was one occasion where Caruso's penchant for clowning came in handy indeed. It was *Bohème* again, in Philadelphia. The tenor, knowing that de Segurola was not feeling up to par that night, jokingly suggested that he'd sing the "Coat Song" in Act IV. When the time came, the basso pulled Caruso to one side and whispered, "Enrico, save me, save me." And so, the tenor sang the basso aria—and many people, it is said, didn't notice.

Caruso loved to joke off stage as well as on, and was possessed of a remarkably facile wit. Some of his humor was elaborately planned, as when he disguised himself as a reporter and met the composer Humperdinck at the pier, asking idiotic questions until he finally took pity on his victim. Often, though, it was spontaneous and still delightful.

In the fall of 1904 he sang in Berlin with tremendous acclaim; as often happened, he was soon accosted by a lady autograph hunter. He asked to see her book, and in it were many names he'd never heard of, all labeled something like "First among world's harpists" or "First mandolinist of Italy." Caruso wrote, "Enrico Caruso, second tenor."

There was a period when, in a mood for self-improvement, the tenor studied the flute, really practicing diligently. One day a man called upon him to demonstrate a recording machine, and as a test Caruso played a short flute solo into the horn. The salesman played it back while the flautist listened intently. When it was over, Caruso said, "Is that how I sound?"

"Yes. Can I sell you the record?"

"No, but I'll sell you the flute."

The final story, one that catches much of the charm of this incredible artist, concerns the time the then N.Y. Police Commissioner Enright called on him at his apartment at the Knickerbocker Hotel to formally present him with a gold badge as a symbol that Caruso was now an honorary New York City policeman. The tenor was delighted.

"Am I now a policeman?"

"You are."

"Can I arrest people?"

"You can."

"Ah," said the great man, "very good. I go now to find Gatti-Casazza."

IN CLOSING

When Enrico Caruso died, in 1921, his passing darkened a little of all the world. What was mourned was more than the simple loss of a gifted musician, a loss like others sustained every year, but rather the end of a particular kind of warmth and excitement, uniquely Caruso. That he died in the full flood of his power added an aura of martyrdom, but even had he lived to retire, the ultimate loss would have been as keenly felt. Only recently, when Lucrezia Bori died many years after leaving the stage, opera-lovers everywhere felt the sudden poignant gap in their universe, a gap less shocking perhaps but no less real than that opened by Caruso or even by the still more dramatic on-stage death of Leonard Warren.

All of these people—Caruso, Bori, the scores more we superficially visited within the preceding chapters, were something more than merely excellent. The peculiar chemistry of opera can transform a singer into a star, to in turn add to the total magic. When that transformation occurs, and only then, opera can and does transcend its basic irrationality. Luckily, the chemistry is a potent one, apparently creating for each generation its necessary crop of prima donnas. Our own, bless it, is a heady crop indeed, but still directly within a continuing tradition. The part of that tradition that we have examined here, the less serious, non-musical, perhaps even unartistic part, is unique to the wedding of theatre and music,

167

making opera just that much more the queen in the arts. Its greatest practitioners have forever been a little removed from the rest of us, a little odd by work-a-day standards, a little wilder, a little closer to the angels. They possess some extra dimension without which a beautiful voice is of only passing interest. To that dimension, to the opera stars that have it, these few passing glances have been dedicated, with much love.

CAST OF CHARACTERS

CAST OF CHARACTERS

ABBEY, HENRY (1846–1896)—American impresario—helped organize Metropolitan in 1883 and was first manager. Lost great sums of money and was replaced by Leopold Damrosch. Returned to share management chores with Schoeffel and Grau (1891–1896).

AKTË, AINO—Soprano, big star in Richard Strauss works in London in first decade of 20th century, but described by New York critics after Metropolitan Juliette in Gounod's *Roméo and Juliette* as "intolerable."

ALBANI, EMMA (1847–1930)—Born Marie Louise Cecilia Lajeunesse, soprano, quite popular in England and Italy. Known best for Eva, Elisabeth, Desdemona. Retired in 1906.

ALBONI, MARIETTA (1823–1894)—One of the greatest of contraltos; pupil of Rossini; star of La Scala for years.

ALDA, FRANCES (1883–1952)—New Zealand-born soprano, married to Gatti-Casazza until 1928. Sang lyric roles at Metropolitan with success from 1908 to 1910, 1911 to 1929 in over 30 roles.

ALVAREZ, ALBERT (1861–1933)—French dramatic tenor; leading star at Paris Opera for years, and one season (1898) at Metropolitan.

AMARA, LUCINE (b. 1927)—American soprano whose career at Metropolitan has seen her progress from Priestess in *Aida* to title role.

ANTHONY, CHARLES—Contemporary, New Orleans-born lyric tenor with lovely voice; advancing on Metropolitan roster from comprimario roles to larger parts.

ARIMONDI, VITTORIO (1861–1928)—Bass, active at variety of local companies (Hammerstein's Manhattan Opera, Metropolitan).

ARMANDI (circa end of the 19th century)—Obscure Italian tenor who gained some small measure of renown by reason of his ineptitude.

ARNOULD, SOPHIE (1740–1802)—Soprano, Parisian favorite for 20 years. Retired in 1770 to become renowned as "wit." Created lead in Gluck's *Iphegenia in Aulis*.

BAMBOSCHEK, GIUSEPPE (b. 1890)—Conductor, assistant to Gatti-Casazza at Metropolitan (1913–1929). Musical director of Philadelphia Grand Opera Company and other opera groups throughout United States.

BARBIROLLI, SIR JOHN (b. 1899)—'Cellist and conductor; one-time head of New York Philharmonic; director Halle Orchestra (Manchester, England) since 1942.

BATTISTINI, MATTIA (1856–1928)—One of outstanding bel canto baritones; flexible voice with easy top. Remained in fine voice until death. Hated ocean travel; never sang in United States.

BEECHAM, SIR THOMAS (1879–1961)—Noted British conductor and sometimes impresario, famed for dexterity with words as well as music.

BELLINI, VINCENZO (1801–1835)—Superbly gifted opera composer; one of the great melodists of all time. *Norma* and *I Puritani* are best-known works. Died tragically young.

BEMBERG, HERMAN—Minor composer, playboy, dilettante around the turn of the century.

BILLINGTON, MRS. ELIZABETH (1768–1818)—Good-looking soprano with 3-octave range. Pupil of J. C. Bach; London favorite.

BING, RUDOLF (b. Vienna, 1902)—General Manager of Metropolitan since 1950, replacing Edward Johnson. Many new productions under his aegis, of varying quality.

BISPHAM, DAVID (1857–1921)—American dramatic baritone; started in oratorio, debuted in opera at Covent Garden; sang there, at Metropolitan and elsewhere with great versatility.

BIZET, GEORGES (1838–1875)—French; composer of *Carmen*, *Pearl Fishers;* tragically short and unhappy life. Brilliant theatre genius.

BODANYA, NATALIE—Second-line soprano at Metropolitan in late 1930's, early 40's. Sang during first Metropolitan Spring season (1935). Did roles like Micaela in *Carmen; The Bartered Bride;* Papagena in *The Magic Flute.*

BODANZKY, ARTUR (1877–1939)—After apprenticeship under Mahler and elsewhere, became chief conductor of Metropolitan's German Wing in 1915.

BOITO, ARRIGO (1842–1918)—Composer of *Mefistofele* and *Nerone;* librettist of *Otello* and *Falstaff.*

BORDONI, FAUSTINA (1693–1781)—Celebrated, highly cultivated mezzo-soprano; star of many of Handel's operas. Married famous tenor Hasse.

BORGATTI, GIUSEPPE (1871–?)—Italian dramatic tenor, who made a fine career throughout Italy, Spain, Russia, created title role in Giordano's *Andrea Chénier;* also noted as Lohengrin, Tristan, Siegfried.

BRAHAM, JOHN (1774–1856)—born Abraham. Noted English tenor with easy skill and 3-octave range; also composed popular ballads.

BRANDT, MARIANNE (1842–1921)—German dramatic contralto; created role of Kundry in Wagner's *Parsifal.* Sang all over, including Metropolitan (1886–1890).

BRIGNOLI—Journeyman tenor, active in the last part of 19th century, toured extensively with Colonel Mapleson and others. Rather wackier than most.

BÜLOW, HANS VON (1830–1893)—Hugely influential conductor; first to conduct extensively without score. Defender of Wagner despite loss of wife (Cosima) to composer.

CAFFARELLI (1703–1783)—Born Gaetano Majorano. Famous castrato, studied 5 years with Poprora; fabulous florid skill, enormous success everywhere except in London.

CALLAS, MARIA (b. 1923)—Stormy petrel of contemporary opera scene; famed for remarkable dramatic sense, wobbly top notes, displays of temperament.

CALVÉ, EMMA (1863–1942)—Tempestuous French soprano, remembered chiefly as Carmen and Santuzza. One of galaxy of Metropolitan stars in decade before Gatti (1893–1907).

CAMPANARI, GIUSEPPE (1858–1927)—Eminent baritone, began as 'cellist (played with Boston Symphony). Sang at Metropolitan (1895–1908).

CAMPANINI, CLEOFONTE (1860–1919)—Operatic conductor, brother of tenor Italo. In pit at Covent Garden, La Scala. Musical director of Hammerstein's Manhattan Opera (1906–1909).

CARELLI, EMMA (1877–1928)—Fine Italian soprano, star at La Scala around turn of century. Colleague of, among others, Caruso.

CARRË, ALBERT (1852–1938)—Director of Opéra Comique 1898–1912. Introduced Charpentier's opera *Louise*.

CARUSO, ENRICO (1873–1921)—Probably best-known of all opera singers. Made Metropolitan debut in 1903 in *Rigoletto*. Sang almost 50 lyric and spinto tenor roles. Voice was in its prime when he died. Created leading tenor roles in *Fedora, Adriana Lecouvreur, Girl of the Golden West*.

CATALANI, ANGELICA (1780–1849)—Famed, beautiful soprano with extraordinary range and flexibility. Nowhere near as successful when she tried running an opera house.

CHALIAPIN, FYODOR (1873–1938)—Marvelous Russian basso; almost as fine an artist as he thought he was. Best-known for his remarkable *Boris*.

CHRISTOFF, BORIS (b. 1919)—Bulgarian basso. Opera debut in 1946 as Pimen in *Boris;* 3 years later sang title role, and became famous as Boris at Covent Garden, La Scala, San Francisco, Chicago.

CLARKE, JOHN—American tenor (late 19th century), who for a time toured with Colonel Mapleson's opera company.

CONREID, HEINRICH (1855–1909)—Impresario in New York from 1878. Took over Metropolitan from Grau in 1901. Gave first non-Bayreuth *Parsifal* (1905); retired in 1908.

CORELLI, FRANCO (b. 1924)—Sensational Italian dramatic tenor; debut 1952; strikingly handsome and high spirited. Metropolitan debut 1961 as Manrico.

CORTI—Late 19th century Italian impresario, apparently handy with his fists.

COSTA, SIR MICHAEL (1808–1884)—Well-known conductor; son and pupil of Pasquale Costa.

CUZZONI, FRANCESCA (1700–1770)—Debuted in 1714. One of most successful contraltos of Handel's day; eked out living later covering buttons with silk.

DE AHNA, PAULINE—Soprano, later wife of Richard Strauss. She (like he) appears as a character in *Intermezzo*. Created role of Freihilde in his opera *Guntram* (1894).

DEBUSSY, CLAUDE (1862–1918)—Impressionist composer; his only opera, *Pelléas et Mélisande*, still controversial, but generally considered a masterpiece.

DELIUS, FREDERICK (1862–1934)—English composer championed by Beecham—individual style—much vocal music including *A Village Romeo and Juliet*.

DE LUCA, GIUSEPPE (1876–1950)—Last of the bel canto baritones, fine singer with long career. Sang at Metropolitan over 800 times. Gave recital as late as 1947. A giant among giants.

DE LUCIA, FERNANDO (1860–1925)—Italian tenor with superb command of the mezza voce, generally excellent technique. He was successful from time of debut in Gounod's *Faust* in Naples in 1883. Sang much in England, United States (at Metropolitan in 1890's in operas like Mascagni's *L'Amico Fritz*).

DE PAOLIS, ALESSIO (b. 1893)—Metropolitan comprimario tenor, fine character performer. Original debut in Rome as leading tenor.

DE RESZKE, EDOUARD (1855–1917)—Basso half of most famed brother act in opera history. Made Metropolitan debut (with Jean) in *Lohengrin*. Left in 1903.

DE RESZKE, JEAN (1850–1925)—One of greatest of all tenors, acknowledged king before Caruso's accession. Idolized in Wagner and in lighter roles; fabulous artist—left Metropolitan in 1901 despite pleas to stay. Brother of Edouard.

DE SEGUROLA, ANDRES (d. 1953)—Spanish basso; took up singing after studying law—sang at Metropolitan 10 years.

DI MURSKA, ILMA (1836–1889)—Noted dramatic soprano, as famed for beautiful 3-octave range as for her odd ways.

DIPPEL, ANDREAS (1866–1932)—American dramatic tenor, impresario. Repertoire of over 150 roles made him Kurt Baum of his day, able to substitute at a minute's notice. At Metropolitan 1898–1908; joint manager with Gatti in 1908–1909.

DONIZETTI, GAETANO (1797–1848)—One of most prolific and gifted of Italian opera composers. *Lucia di Lammermoor* most popular work, but wrote 66 other operas, including some great comedies.

DOWNES, OLIN (1891-1955)—Widely read music critic of *The New York Times* from 1924 to death.

DUCHÈNE, MARIA—Mezzo-soprano, at Metropolitan Opera for few years beginning with season of 1909-10. Did roles like Ulrica, etc.

EAMES, EMMA (1865-1952)—Shanghai-born American diva; reigning star at Metropolitan for two decades, 1891-1909. Resigned in pique at Gatti.

FANCELLI, GIUSEPPE (1835-1888)—Badly schooled tenor who achieved opera stardom despite bad musicianship, no color, and a total lack of dramatic ability, but with a fabulously beautiful and accurate voice. Sang with Mapleson Company for years, also sang Radames when Verdi's *Aida* got its first Italian production.

FARRAR, GERALDINE (b. 1882)—One of most adored of American sopranos, with legions of "Gerry-flapper" followers. Sang Juliette, Carmen, Thaïs, Manon, Tosca and many other roles at Metropolitan from 1906 to 1922.

FARRELL, EILEEN (b. 1920)—One of the greatest American sopranos. Blessed with extraordinarily beautiful voice, fine technique, musicality and volume. Started in radio; finally debuted at Metropolitan (*Alcestis*) in 1960. Able to sing well in wide variety of roles.

FRANCHETTI, BARON ALBERTO (1860-1942)—Composer; born wealthy; first opera most successful (*Asrael*), others now fading despite his real talents.

FREMSTAD, OLIVE (1846-1951)—Great and colorful Swedish-American soprano; one of finest Wagnerians, sang at Metropolitan from 1903-1914. Known for dramatic ability and great beauty as well as voice.

GABRIELLI, CATARINA (1730-1796)—Daughter of Prince Gabrielli's cook, thus called "La Cochettina"; capricious, picturesque soprano with great skill and incredibly lovely voice.

GABRIELLI, FRANCESCA (1755-1795)—Sister of Catarina, called "La Gabriellina"; was celebrated soprano buffa.

GADSKI, JOHANNA (1871-1932)—Noted Wagnerian soprano with large, dramatic voice; rival of Fremstad. A leading artist of Metropolitan 1898–1917, when her pro-German sentiments forced her out.

GALLI-CURCI, AMELITA (b. 1889)—One of finest coloraturas of the century; certainly one of the most adored. Sang at Chicago opera 1916–1924, Metropolitan 1921–1930. Known as Gilda, Violetta, etc.

GARCIA, MANUEL (1775–1832)—Eminent Spanish vocal teacher as well as superb tenor, conductor, composer, impresario, father of Maria Malibran, Pauline Viardot-Garcia, Manuel Jr. Teacher of Jenny Lind and many others.

GARDEN, MARY (b. 1877)—Glamorous soprano star; created role of Mélisande; famous for work in French opera generally. Managed Chicago opera for one season.

GATTI-CASAZZA, GIULIO (1869–1940)—Born in Italy. Impresario of Metropolitan 1908–1935. Brought Toscanini with him to Metropolitan. Married briefly to Frances Alda, a Metropolitan prima donna; later to prima ballerina Rosina Galli.

GERSTER, ETELKA (1855–1920)—Great Hungarian coloratura soprano; rival of Patti; diva of the old school. Toured America with Mapleson. Left stage in 1890 to found singing school in Berlin.

GIGLI, BENIAMINO (1890–1957)—Italian lyric tenor; extraordinarily sweet and pure tone. Sang all over world with huge success, although his endorsement of Fascism eclipsed his career for a while. Perhaps finest of lyrics of 1920's and 30's. At Metropolitan 1920–1932.

GIORDANO, UMBERTO (1867–1948)—Composer of many operas, most popular of which is *Andrea Chénier*.

GIUGLINI, ANTONIO (1827–1865)—Italian tenor, noted for roles like Arturo, Edgardo, Manrico, popular in London, where he debuted in *La Favorita* by Donizetti. Died insane.

GLUCK, CHRISTOPH WILLIBALD (1714–1787)—"Great Reformer" of opera from vocal excesses of predecessors; composer of *Orfeo ed Euridice*, *Alceste*, etc.

GOUNOD, CHARLES (1818–1893)—French composer, savant; most remembered today for the ubiquitous *Faust*, but wrote a flock of other operas.

GRASSINI, GIUSEPPINA (1773–1850)—Willful, extraordinarily beautiful and talented soprano; sang throughout musical world with great success.

GRAU, MAURICE (1849–1907)—Last of the pre-Gatti Metropolitan impresarios, credited with discovering Caruso.

GRISI, GIULIA (1811–1869)—Biggest soprano star of her time; from musical family; debut, Milan, 1828; retired 1867; married tenor Mario. Admired by Bellini, Rossini, Donizetti. Sister and pupil of Giuditta Grisi.

GUDEHUS, HEINRICH (1845–1909)—Tenor, often appeared in Wagnerian roles. Created Parsifal at Bayreuth. Sang at Metropolitan in 1890's.

HAMMERSTEIN, OSCAR (1846–1919)—Fabled German-born showman who successfully challenged the Metropolitan for a few seasons at the Manhattan Opera House with his own opera company (1906–1910).

HAUK, MINNIE (1851–1929)—American soprano. Made debut at 14 in *La Sonnambula*. Her fiery interpretation of Carmen won this opera new popularity. Created role in 1878 for England and United States. Sang it over 600 times in four languages. Despite success, died blind and poverty-stricken.

HIGGINS, SIR ARTHUR—Manager of Covent Garden Opera Company during the great days of Scotti and Caruso.

ILLICA, LUIGI (1857–1919)—Italian librettist; wrote books for Catalani's *La Wally*, Giordano's *Andrea Chénier*; collaborated On Puccini's *La Bohème, Tosca, Madama Butterfly, Manon Lescaut*.

JERITZA, MARIA (b. 1887)—Tempestuous soprano star of Vienna, Metropolitan, after start in operetta. Renowned for dramatic powers in roles such as Tosca, Turandot and the Strauss roles. At Metropolitan 1921–1932.

JÖRN, KARL (1876–1947)—Latvian tenor; sang throughout Europe; at Metropolitan 1908–1911.

KAHN, OTTO (1867–1934)—Most famous of modern patrons of music; 1908–1931 Chairman of Board of Metropolitan and for years dominated its policies. Generously supported many causes, but loved Metropolitan best of all.

KALISCH, PAUL (1855–?)—German tenor, husband of the formidable Lilli Lehmann, by whom he was dominated. Sang with her in Berlin and in United States.

KELLOGG, CLARA LOUISE (1842–1916)—First true American prima donna; trained in New York; debuted there in 1861. Marguerite in *Faust* most noted role.

KELLY, MICHAEL (1764–1826)—Tenor, friend of Mozart, about whom he wrote extensively in *Reminiscences.* Took part in première of *Marriage of Figaro.*

KIEPURA, JAN (b. 1902)—Polish tenor—began opera career in Vienna. At Metropolitan 1938–1942; known best as the suitor to wife Martha Eggerth in *Merry Widow.*

KOUSSEVITZKY, SERGE (1874–1951)—Great conductor of Boston Symphony during its glory years (1924–51). Champion of new music; founder of Berkshire Music Festival.

KURZ, SELMA (1875–1933)—Austrian coloratura headquartered in Vienna where she was a favorite for over a quarter-century. Had fine trill; appeared with Vienna Opera throughout Europe.

LA BLACHE, EMILY—Well-regarded contralto, who sang for both Henry Abbey and Maurice Grau around the turn of the century.

LaBLACHE, LUIGI (1794–1858)—Great basso; rich, flexible voice, one of original *Puritani* quartet. Considered by many greatest buffo of all time, as well as fine serious basso.

LAWRENCE, MARJORIE (b. 1907)—Australian dramatic soprano; debuted 1935 at Metropolitan; recognized as great Wagnerian 'till suddenly struck down by polio in 1941. With remarkable courage returned to Metropolitan still paralyzed, to sing Venus and Isolde. Movie of her life, *Interrupted Melody*—1955.

LE BLANC, GEORGETTE (d. 1941)—Soprano; starred at (Paris) Opera from time of 1893 debut. Afterwards noted for recitals in costume.

LEHMANN, LILLI (1848–1929)—Grande dame of German opera in decades before 1900; wide repertoire, fabulous technique; awesome self-assurance. Starred at Metropolitan in its early days.

LEHMANN, LOTTE (b. 1885)—Superb German lyric-dramatic soprano; highly acclaimed at Metropolitan, Vienna and elsewhere. Created role of composer in *Ariadne auf Naxos;* famous in Strauss, Wagner and as Lieder singer. Still active as "master coach."

LEONCAVALLO, RUGGIERO (1858–1919)—Composer of one marvelous work (libretto too), *Pagliacci,* and a succession of pretentious bores.

LIND, JENNY (1820–1887)—"Swedish Nightingale"—perhaps most popular soprano in history. Sang everywhere; toured United States under auspices of P. T. Barnum.

LOWE, MARIE—Mother of Lilli Lehmann and excellent soprano in her own right. Also noted as a distinguished harpist. Original heroine of several Spohr operas.

MAETERLINCK, MAURICE (1864–1949)—Nobel Laureate (1911) for Literature; wrote play on which Debussy's *Pelléas et Mélisande* is based.

MAHLER, GUSTAV (1860–1911)—Brilliant gifted conductor, composer; his genius only now being adequately appreciated. Conducted at Metropolitan, New York Philharmonic, Vienna State Opera.

MALIBRAN, MARIA (1808–1836)—Considered by many the greatest female vocalist of all time—range from deep contralto to high soprano. Daughter and pupil of Manuel Garcia—huge success musically and dramatically till early death.

MAPLESON, COLONEL JAMES H. (1830–1901)—Impresario, hard-pressed but successful. Introduced many operas and singers; based in England; toured United States frequently.

MARCHESI, MATHILDE (1821–1913)—Pupil of Manuel Garcia, Jr. One of great vocal teachers of all times; taught dozens from Melba to Eames.

MARIO, GIUSEPPE (1810–1883)—Born Conte di Candia; eminent and adored tenor, one of most famed of time. Husband of Giulia Grisi.

MASINI, ANGELO (1845–?)—During his prime regarded as the Premier Tenor in Italy, Tamagno's big rival. Sang in first Paris *Aida* with Verdi himself conducting (1876).

MASSENET, JULES (1842–1912)—Eminent French opera composer, noted for excellent melodic facility and true Gallic flavor —*Manon*, many others.

MATERNA, AMALIE (1845–1918)—Soprano, prima donna of Vienna Court Opera—1864–1896. First Bayreuth Brünnhilde.

MAUREL, VICTOR (1848–1923)—Eminent baritone; created roles of Iago and Falstaff. Famous as foremost dramatic artist of his time.

MAZZOLENI—19th century Italian tenor, character in Clara Louise Kellogg's memoirs.

McCORMACK, JOHN (1884–1945)—Lyric tenor; fine in opera, but scored hugest success in concert; one of most popular recitalists in history.

MELBA, NELLIE (Australian, 1859–1931)—One of most adored and idolized sopranos of turn of century. Debut 1887; farewell, Covent Garden, 1926. Possessed lovely silvery voice.

MELCHIOR, LAURITZ (b. 1890)—Danish Heldentenor, perhaps greatest of all time despite unorthodox vocal production. Began as baritone. Metropolitan debut 1926. Left after Bing came.

MERRILL, ROBERT (b. 1919)—Brooklyn-born owner of most beautiful baritone voice of day; won Metropolitan auditions, 1945; debuted in *La Traviata;* since has sung there as one of its leading artists.

MESSAGER, ANDRÉ (1853–1929)—Composer and impresario —musical director Covent Garden 1901–1907. Director of Paris Opera 1907–1919; Opéra Comique, 1919–1920.

MEYERBEER, GIACOMO (1791–1864)—Became most successful and popular composer of his time after years of trying and studying. *Robert le Diable* broke the ice, followed by *Les Huguenots, Le Prophète, L'Africaine,* etc.

MONTEMEZZI, ITALO (1875–1952)—Italian opera composer, remembered chiefly for *L'Amore dei Tre Re* (The Love of Three Kings.)

MONTEVERDI, CLAUDIO (1567–1643)—First great operatic composer, often credited with development of true aria. Wrote *Orfeo, Coronation of Poppea.*

MOORE, GRACE (1901–1947)—American soprano, started in musical comedy; then trained for opera. Metropolitan debut 1928; great favorite. Later returned to musicals, films. Killed in plane crash.

MORELL, BARRY (b. 1927)—New York-born lyric tenor; started career at New York City Opera, graduated to Metropolitan; well-schooled, attractive voice; excellent Pinkerton, Rodolfo, Duke, etc.

MUCK, KARL (1859–1940)—Distinguished conductor, including (before World War I) Boston Symphony.

MUGNONE, LEOPOLDO (1858–?)—Noted conductor of opera including Wagner, and the première of Verdi's *Falstaff.*

NASOLINI, SEBASTIANO (1768–?)—Produced over 30 operas in Italy.

NEVADA, EMMA (1862–1940)—American soprano, born Emma Wixom. Pupil of Mathilde Marchesi. Debut, London, 1880. Sang in Italy, Paris, America for two decades.

NICOLINI, ERNEST (1834–1898)—Tenor, married Adelina Patti, but otherwise rather undistinguished.

NIEMANN, ALBERT (1831–1917)—Great dramatic tenor, created *Tannhäuser* in Paris; star of first Bayreuth *Ring*. Arrogant, gifted.

NIKISCH, ARTUR (1855–1922)—Eminent conductor, one of the first of the "virtuoso" conductors; widely renowned, especially as head of Berlin and London Philharmonic Orchestras.

NILSSON, BIRGIT—Contemporary Swedish dramatic soprano with stunning top register; noted for Wagnerian roles, Turandot, etc.

NILSSON, CHRISTINE (1843–1921)—Swedish soprano, sang Marguerite in *Faust* which opened the Metropolitan in 1883.

NORDICA, LILLIAN (1859–1914)—American soprano, remembered mostly for Wagnerian roles, but sang others too. Big Metropolitan star around turn of century.

PATTI, ADELINA (1843–1919)—Debut in United States at age 17; most celebrated diva of her time, especially in coloratura roles. Last concert (except for benefits) 1906.

PINZA, EZIO (1892–1957)—Adored basso, at Metropolitan from 1926 till he succumbed to lure of Broadway. Was reason for Metropolitan's Mozart revivals in 1930's. Famous as Don Giovanni, Boris, and in Verdi roles.

PLANCON, POL (1854–1914)—Sensational French basso, noted for *Faust* Méphistophélès at Metropolitan 1893–1908—fine technique. Like others, he left when Gatti came.

POLACCO, GIORGIO (1875–1960)—Much loved operatic conductor; Metropolitan debut 1912; Chicago Opera from 1922 to retirement in 1930.

PONS, LILY (b. 1904)—French coloratura; began as piano student; debuted sensationally as high soprano at Metropolitan in *Lucia*, 1931, her arrival heralding rash of revivals. American citizen in 1940. Charm, beauty, voice all made her genuine star.

PONSELLE, ROSA (b. 1894)—American dramatic soprano, owner of fabulously beautiful voice; debut at Metropolitan 1918 in *Forza del Destino*. Reigned there till retirement in 1937. One of the greats without question; biggest triumph as Norma, revived for her in 1927. She especially loved Carmen which she first sang in 1935.

PUCCINI, GIACOMO (1858–1924)—One of the most gifted melodists in operatic history, able to strike to heart of emotions. First success *Manon Lescaut* (Turin, 1893), last, *Turandot*, remained unfinished at death.

RANKIN, NELL (b. 1926)—From Montgomery, Alabama, American dramatic mezzo-soprano with unusually long range up to spectacular high C. Best known throughout Europe and America for mezzo leads in Verdi operas and *Carmen,* and for Ortrud in *Lohengrin*.

RAVELLI, LUIGI—Italian tenor, one of the more difficult ones. Made his debut with Mapleson's Opera Company in 1881.

REEVES, SIMS (1818–1900)—Noted tenor, starred at number of London theatres for decades after switching from baritone.

REINHOLD, EVA—Soprano, teacher. Member—not a very perceptive one, apparently—of faculty of Etelka Gerster's Singing School in Berlin during early decades of 20th century.

RICH, JOHN (1682–1761)—London impresario, manager of an Opera Company that starred Mrs. Tofts; producer of John Gay's *The Beggar's Opera*.

ROSSINI, GIOACCHINO (1792–1868)—Prolific and brilliant composer with rich comic sense. Last opera, *William Tell*, 1829. Rossini, then 37, lived 39 more years without writing another opera.

ROZE, MARIE (1846–1926)—French soprano, scored great success in London in 70's and 80's.

RUBINI, GIOVANNI (1795–1854)—Almost legendary tenor, said to have introduced vibrato and the sob. Favorite of Bellini; so popular he amassed incredible fortune.

RUBINSTEIN, ANTON (1829–1894)—One of world's greatest pianists; something less than that as composer. Wrote many operas, mostly forgotten now.

RUSSELL, HENRY (1871–1937)—Renowned English teacher and impresario. From 1909 to 1914 director of resurgent Boston Opera.

RYLOFF—Belgian conductor, middle of nineteenth century.

SAINT-SAËNS, CAMILLE (1835–1921)—Eminent composer; at one time highly influential but now increasingly forgotten. Perhaps best known now for *Samson et Dalila*.

SALVINI-DONATELLI, FANNY (mid 19th century)—Corpulent but gifted soprano, the second wife of famous tragedian Tommaso Salvini. Created role of Violetta in world première of Verdi's *La Traviata*.

SAMMONS, ALBERT (b. 1886)—Noted violinist; concert master for Beecham for a time.

SARATA, ALBERTO—Italian impresario, manager of the Milan Grand Italian Opera Company which played in America occasionally in last part of 19th century.

SCALCHI, SOFIA (1850–1919)—Italian mezzo-soprano. Toured United States with Mapleson. In cast of opening night *Faust* at Metropolitan in 1883. Retired in 1896.

SCHEFF, FRITZI (1879–1954)—Viennese soprano. Biggest triumphs on Broadway, but earliest successes in opera. Debuted in 1897; at Metropolitan 1900–1903, when she abandoned opera for Victor Herbert.

SCHUMANN, ELISABETH (1891–1952)—Delightful German lyric, Sophie to Lotte Lehmann's Marschallin in most famed *Rosenkavalier* cast. Hamburg, Vienna, Metropolitan star, Lieder singer of renown. Toured with Richard Strauss.

SCHUMANN-HEINK, ERNESTINE (1861–1936)—Great and much-beloved German contralto. Sang Italian and German opera. Made Metropolitan debut in 1899. Sang there on and off till 1932, when she sang Erda at age 71.

SCOTTI, ANTONIO (1866–1936)—Leading Metropolitan baritone for 35 years. Master actor, great friend of Caruso. Sang American premières of six operas including *Tosca*. Best known as Scarpia.

SEMBRICH, MARCELLA (1858–1935)—Polish soprano; turned to singing on advice of Liszt; debut 1877. Great vocal agility led to acclaim. Leading star at Metropolitan 'till 1909.

SENGER-BETTAQUE, KATHARINA (1862–?)—Soprano; started career as ballerina, later became soubrette, later still turned to Wagner.

SLEZAK, LEO (1875–1946)—Great tenor; studied with De Reszke; starred as Otello, in Wagner, etc. in many companies (Metropolitan 1909–1913), particularly Vienna.

SOEDERSTROEM, ELISABETH (b. 1927)—Contemporary Swedish lyric soprano, star of Swedish Royal Opera and Metropolitan; lovely voice and appearance, fine acting skill, great charm. Excels in comic roles (Susanna, Adina) as well as tragic (Marguerite, Mimi, Madama Butterfly).

STEBER, ELEANOR (b. 1916)—American soprano star of Metropolitan since debut in 1940 after winning Auditions of the Air. Finest Mozart and Strauss soprano produced in United States. Also sings Verdi, Puccini, Wagner, etc.

STEVENS, RISË (b. 1913)—American mezzo-soprano; made Metropolitan debut 1938. Striking looks and personality made her a top star, particularly as Carmen, Octavian. Also active in movies.

STIGELLI—19th century Italian tenor, remembered now chiefly as a character in Clara Louise Kellogg's memoirs.

STRAKOSCH, MAURICE (1825–1887)—Famed impresario, pianist and teacher. Taught Adelina Patti, and married her sister Carlotta.

STRAUSS, RICHARD (1864–1949)—Last giant among operatic composers; later works underestimated, largely because of World War II, but now being rediscovered as the masterworks they are. Most popular still *Salome, Der Rosenkavalier.*

SUTHERLAND, JOAN (b. 1926)—Australian soprano leggiero who, after some undistinguished work in the dramatic repertoire, zoomed to stardom in a Covent Garden *Lucia di Lammermoor.* Has since repeated triumph in other florid roles in England, United States, Italy—fine technique; fabulous trill.

SVANHOLM, SET (b. 1904)—Swedish Heldentenor; short-term successor to Melchior at Metropolitan—fine musician, small stature. Now first-rate head of Swedish Royal Opera.

TAMAGNO, FRANCESCO (1850–1905)—Brilliant Italian tenor famed for clarion tone and stentorian power. Chosen by Verdi to create role of Otello.

TAMBURINI, ANTONIO (1800–1876)—Fabulous baritone, one of the famed *Puritani* quartet. Said to have been one of the finest male vocalists.

TAUBER, RICHARD (1892–1948)—Born Ernst Seiffert—renowned lyric tenor, equally beloved in opera and operetta throughout Germany, Austria, France and England.

TEBALDI, RENATA (b. 1922)—Magnificent Italian lyricospinto, best loved for her portrayals of Puccini heroines. Sings throughout Europe and America. Made Metropolitan debut in 1955 as Desdemona.

TETRAZZINI, LUISA (1871–1940)—One of greatest coloraturas of all time. Sang all over world; only one year at Metropolitan. Last appearance here 1931. Very popular.

TEYTE, MAGGIE (b. 1890)—English soprano; studied with Jean De Reszke, debut 1907; sang with many opera companies; last with New York City Opera as Mélisande.

TIBBETT, LAWRENCE (1896–1960)—Baritone; leaped to stardom while singing Ford in *Falstaff* at Metropolitan after inconspicuous beginnings. Dominated Metropolitan's baritone wing between Scotti and Warren, fine actor.

TITIENS (also TIETJENS), THÉRÈSE (1831–1877)—Soprano; popular favorite in London from 1858. A favorite of Bellini.

TOFTS, MRS. CATHERINE (d. 1756)—English soprano, first to sing Italian opera on her home soil. Her success bred a remarkable passion for money, as well as some delusions of grandeur.

TOSCANINI, ARTURO (1867–1957)—Fiery perfectionist; considered by many the greatest conductor of the century. Particularly gifted in opera, conducted at La Scala and Metropolitan.

TOSTI, PAOLO (1846–1916)—Famous baritone, teacher, composer of songs.

TOZZI, GIORGIO (b. 1923)—Chicago-born basso with marvelously warm, sonorous voice and admirable technique. Leading star of Metropolitan, many recordings, well-loved in Europe as well as America. Began career in musical comedy, to which he occasionally returns.

TRAUBEL, HELEN (b. 1899)—Metropolitan debut 1937. Powerful dramatic soprano; one of finest Wagnerians produced in United States despite fading top notes. Left Metropolitan after Bing came.

VAN CAUTEREN, MARIE—Minor turn-of-the-century mezzosoprano; sang roles like the Marquise in Donizetti's *Daughter of the Regiment* at Metropolitan.

VAN DYCK, ERNEST (1861–1923)—Noted Belgian dramatic tenor; turned to vocal career after law and journalism; sang Wagner, some French opera. At Metropolitan, 1898–1902. Big star in Vienna and throughout Europe.

VAN ZANDT, MARIE (1861–1919)—American soprano, created role of Lakmé. Debut 1879. Sang briefly at Metropolitan, but greatest success was in Paris.

VERDI, GIUSEPPE (1813–1901)—Towering operatic genius, getting, if anything, better as he got older. Wrote *Otello* at 73; *Falstaff* at 79.

VIARDOT-GARCIA, PAULINE (1812–1910)—Soprano, daughter of Manuel Garcia; 3-octave range—sang mezzo roles—created Fides in *Le Prophète*.

VOTIPKA, THELMA—Beloved soprano comprimario of Metropolitan for many years. Still very active.

WAGNER, COSIMA (1837–1930)—Second wife of composer Richard; divorced wife of Hans von Bülow and natural daughter of Liszt; as widow, ruled Bayreuth with iron hand.

WAGNER, RICHARD (1813–1883)—Moody genius; creator of towering musical masterpieces and much philosophical drivel. For a generation his music was a cause célèbre both for and against. Probably single most influential opera composer.

WALSKA, GANNA—Polish would-be soprano; through great personal wealth she subsidized several opera companies in Paris and United States in return for privilege of "singing" which she seldom exercised.

WARREN, LEONARD (1911–1960)—American baritone; sang at Radio City Music Hall before winning Metropolitan auditions on a dare; debut 1940; was leading Metropolitan star, constantly improving, until his stunning on-stage death midway through big aria in *La Forza del Destino*.

WELITCH, LJUBA (b. 1913)—Bulgarian soprano, active mostly in Vienna. Scored sensational triumph as Salome at Metropolitan in 1949. Also sang Verdi roles, Tosca etc., till strain on voice showed.

ZENATELLO, GIOVANNI (1879–1949)—Popular tenor; among other places he starred at Hammerstein's Manhattan Opera Company, 1907–09.